Weekly
ENCOURAGEMENTS

by

NAUM WARE

ISBN 978-1-64471-364-8 (Paperback)
ISBN 978-1-64471-365-5 (Digital)

Covenant Books, Inc.
11661 Hwy 707
Murrells Inlet, SC 29576
www.covenantbooks.com

Faith Worth Finding Ministries with Naum Ware

Hannah's Humility

Part 1

Do you feel you have missed out on something important in life and it is heartbreaking? You want to be married, you wanted to marry someone else; you wanted a different career? In these moments and others like them, the amount of faith we have in God will be severely tested because the things we want most in life, God hasn't given us and we know that He can.

So many incidents in our lives emerge defining who we really are. It gets to the point where we cannot separate what we do all the time and who we've become. We are defined by our actions—a defining moment if you please.

Now the question comes to mind: can we get success out of what looks to be apparent failure? Can we make where we're challenged work for us? That is what Hannah did, that is why we want to talk about Hannah's humility.

Don't ever assume you're the only one who is having difficulty or unfulfilled dreams or desires. Nobody knows the trouble I see, nobody knows my sorrow… (Sound familiar)?

We must stop looking at others with a cocked eye because they already have what we desire. Stop feeling cheated because you don't have what you have longed for so long.

All of us want something we don't have; it's human nature. A married person wants to be financially successful. A single person who is already financially successful wants to be married. Gifted genius students want to be athletic, while athletic students wish they were smarter. Good-looking or beautiful people wish they had some self-esteem; while regular looking folk wish they were more attractive. You see the experience of unfulfillment is universal, regardless of our color, marital status, social standing, or financial bracket.

In Hannah's case, she had complete devotion from her husband Elkanah. His other wife, Peninnah, knew she was second fiddle. But Peninnah could give Elkanah children to carry on his name; this was critical to Hebrew culture. Hannah on the other hand could not. So it was common back then for a man to take on one wife he loved, then another for children. For Hannah, it was painful because she loved her husband. Not only so Peninnah had numerous children.

Elkannah did his best to show Hannah he loved her. He gave her a double portion of the sacrificial meal as if to say, "I love you twice as much, even without kids. I love you for you; not for the children you can give me."

Most women would be overjoyed to have a husband so devoted to them, so tender and compassionate. Hannah was grateful, but she wanted a child. Until she had one, she felt horribly unfulfilled.

Now of course Peninnah witnessed all this love and devotion and became jealous so she hit Hannah where it hurt. Peninnah taunted Hannah for her inability to conceive; this made Hannah not even want to go to the Temple anymore. Few things are more painful than knowing God can remove our pain and fulfill our dreams, but He chooses not to do so.

Hannah was not the only one with desires. Peninnah wanted Elkanah's devotion and love as much as Hannah wanted children. You see, our world is full of people who feel inadequate and incomplete. They are chasing an elusive dream. *Here is the key; our attitude in these moments is what will truly define us.*

We are tempted to blame or abandon God, or have cheap substitutes. But this is where Hannah shines brightly, and why the Holy Spirit chose her life story for our encouragement.

Unfulfillment is not a punishment from God. It can feel that way; like God is grounding us. Hannah must have struggled with this. In her culture, barrenness was a sign of personal failure and seemingly a punishment from God. When her family went to the Tabernacle to give their peace offerings, a portion of the meat was given to each family member. Hannah had to sit and watch as Peninnah gave a portion to each of her children. It was a constant reminder to Hannah of her perceived inadequacies as a woman and a wife.

You ever felt that way—unfulfilled? Are you lacking what someone else has ample supply of? Do you feel like God is punishing you? Are you in continual financial distress or have you seen others advancing in their careers while you atrophy or stagnate? Do you have a spouse? Does your spouse not love you like you need? All of this can be painful and make us feel inadequate. *We may very well be tempted to accuse God of unfairness and withhold our worship.* These normal human tendencies make Hannah's actions all the more commendable.

Peninnah provided us with a stark contrast to Hannah's attitude. Peninnah assumed and concluded that her children were a personal accomplishment and not a blessing from the Lord. She tormented Hannah over her predicament. She flaunted her own favorable situation and treated God's blessings as a personal triumph. Peninnah's taunts insinuated that she believed she was more loved by God than Hannah because she had children and Hannah didn't.

But Hannah understood that her dilemma was not God's punishment. We know this because her prayer at the temple. She didn't confess any sin to God she simply kept asking Him to give her what was withheld. It was an uncomplicated honest prayer, wholehearted and fervent. You could feel her pain and seriousness. Her hope and faith shined in this prayer. I want to point out a few things I observed clearly in this prayer.

1 Samuel 1:11

1. Hannah didn't mind praying for something God might never fulfill. I hope you're not missing this. I want you to fully grasp what Hannah is promising. Hannah was willing to give up the very thing she most wanted. She wanted a son and promised to make him a Nazarite for life; to dedicate him to God's service. Hebrew women traditionally weaned their children at three years old; this means Hannah would give up her three-year-old to service in the temple of God if God would bless her with a son.

This was purely *humble* and *unselfish*. Hannah wasn't making a deal with God, "If you do this, I will do this." She was committed to glorifying God with anything He gave her and especially a son. Hannah felt like for her to conceive it would have to be act of God so why not give the gift back to Him in gratitude to glorify Him? Wow!

This was not a flippant decision this was commitment to God and humility.

Three years of age and with no promise she would ever have another child. Do you realize how that child might cling to her, but she would have to let him go at three years old? Wow!

This is what is amazing about Hannah. In her most defining moment, after praying for a son whom she probably prayed for hundreds of times before; at her lowest point, almost despairing, what does she do? *She goes again to God.* Just because He hasn't acted yet doesn't mean He won't. We're talking about faith, hope, and humility.

This wasn't any fuzzy or fussy prayers either; Hannah wanted a baby, a son, who would remove her shame and feelings of inadequacy and incompleteness. She wanted to nurse him, love him, laugh with him, play with him, and then give him to God in thanksgiving. She wanted this so much in so until it was tearing her up inside.

Hannah wasn't asking for money or material things or someone's spouse or instant beauty or even a talent transformation. (James 4:3 talks about this.) Our motivation in that type prayer is not to the glory of God but luxury and pleasure. This was a natural desire of a married woman. There was nothing selfish or sinful in this prayer.

So many times we're often afraid to pray specifically because we don't want to be disappointed when it does not show up in our timetable. God may say no! He may say, not right now! Hannah gave

God the option of saying no and still being her God, still being the One she would worship. (I can't wait for part 2).

God bless you,
Fwfm:nlw

Faith Worth Finding Ministries with Naum Ware

Hannah's Humility

Part 2

I wonder if we could pray the way Hannah did. "Lord, I pray with all my heart. I pray for _____, but if I don't get it; You will still be my God, and I will still love and serve you." That's humility.

What if God had not given Hannah the answer she wanted? Would she have remained faithful? Yes, she would have. How do we know? Because that is exactly what had been happening year after year. Yearly she returned again and again with faith strong enough to believe He could do this thing for her, and her love for Him strong enough to accept a "no"! This strong faith carries Hannah in her darkest days. Even when she failed to get her request, she did not blame God.

Secondly Hannah taught us to *never give God an ultimatum.* Hannah never did this consciously or unwittingly. Before she prayed, after saying what she had to say to Eli, she ate and then prayed (1 Sam. 1:9, 10). Did you notice her prayer in verse 11? *⁹So Hannah rose up after they had eaten in Shiloh, and after they had drunk. Now Eli the priest sat upon a seat by a post of the temple of the LORD. ¹⁰And she was in bitterness of soul, and prayed unto the LORD, and wept sore. ¹¹And she vowed a vow, and said, O LORD of hosts, if thou wilt indeed look on the affliction of thine handmaid, and remember me, and not forget thine handmaid, but wilt give unto thine handmaid a man child, then I will give him unto the LORD all the days of his life, and there shall no razor come upon his head.*

I wanted to let you see it from KJV, then I wanted you to view in The Message so it can stand out.

9–11 So Hannah ate. Then she pulled herself together, slipped away quietly, and entered the sanctuary. The priest Eli was on duty at the entrance to God*'s Temple in the customary seat. Crushed in soul, Hannah prayed to God and cried and cried—inconsolably. Then she made a vow:*

> *Oh, God-of-the-Angel-Armies,*
> *If you'll take a good, hard look at my pain,*
> *If you'll quit neglecting me and go into action for me*
> *By giving me a son,*
> *I'll give him completely, unreservedly to you.*
> *I'll set him apart for a life of holy discipline.*

Hannah fully recognized that God was under no obligation to provide her with a son. He would still be God, full of love, mercy, and righteousness even if she did not receive her deepest desire. How about you?

So even though Hannah still had no baby and no promise of one, her appetite returned and she was encouraged. All Eli did was offer a general prayer requesting God to bless her with children. It wasn't a prophecy, yet Hannah's faith had been strengthened by the smallest token and she put her life in God's hands to do whatever He would.

You know many times that is when our greatest peace comes; not when we get what we want most, but when we finally and completely place the issue in God's care and we're fully prepared to accept whatever answer He may give.

If we place God under obligation to give us what we want or desire, we create a situation in which God becomes our ATM or servant who exists only to serve our wish or command. God is no genie. Hannah didn't do it and we need to learn from her. *She treated God with reverence and love, happy to serve Him whole heartedly with or without a child.*

The next thing we learn from Hannah is to *let nothing come between you and God.*

When God doesn't answer your prayer in the time frame or manner you want do not move away from Him in disappointment. We do this so often and become cynical. We even stop asking for anything important. A subtle wound develops and we sort of figure; what's the point, why even ask? Hmm.

We even conclude that despite the scripture saying in Romans 8:28, Hebrews 13:5, 6, Psalm 46:1, and so many others, somehow we conclude that God doesn't have our best interest at heart. We allow disappointment to become sand in our eyes or sugar in the engine of our souls.

Hannah's unfulfilled desire, which was a daily burden, actually drew her closer to God (1 Sam. 1:10). Hannah just continued what she was in the habit of doing. This prepared her for her defining moment.

She refused and resisted the urge to react on an aching desire. She also refused to allow herself to grow bitter toward God even though her "feelings" were hurt. She grew silent due to pain in her heart, but she grew closer to God and just kept asking Him for help.

I'm reminded of so many people I've seen climbing the ladder fast in their company, even in church. They are told by others they are on a fast track to get to the top of their profession. Then something happens and they become stagnant at a certain level. They grow weary and discouraged. This happened to one youth pastor who was told he would be the next pastor and when it didn't happen he actually fell into sin.

Call it petting his wounds or whatever, but he became so dismayed or put out until his recourse of recovery was to taste a little sin. Wow!

So that is the answer when you don't get your way; to become eroded and lose your devotion to God thereby affecting your relationship and growth? Maybe that is why you didn't make it because God knew your heart anyway. (I added that in there, forgive me.)

In contrast, this is where Hannah stands out as such a shining example. Hidden deep in Hannah was the defining factor of letting nothing come between her and God. Hannah's faithfulness to God did not go unrewarded and neither will ours. Does this mean we are going to get everything we want, no! It very well may mean that God will change our hearts desire rather than fulfill it-nevertheless we will bless Him.

You have to love God more than you love your personal desire. That is why still today we can discuss Hannah. What a remarkable moment. She loved God even more than she loved her first born, Samuel. We know this because she did the ultimate act of trust.

3

Hannah did something that never could have been accomplished otherwise. Watch this; now don't miss it. In 1 Samuel 2:1–11, look at Hannah's prayer of thanksgiving. Did you know this was prayed before she had any other children and after she had dedicated her baby to God by giving him to Eli the priest? Hannah gave away her most precious possession then prayed this prayer.

It showed that Hannah's praise to God was more precious than the wonderful gift He had given to her. Wow! She didn't even know if she would even have more children and yet she gave up Samuel. What helped Hannah make this choice; she loved God with all her heart. It is only when we love God that we are able to accept any answer from Him and still bless Him.

What about you; do you love God that way or are you disappointed and angry your dreams have not been fulfilled? Have you subconsciously really left God? Let's talk, I'm talking about your actions; not your pious speech. I'm talking about what you possess not what you profess. How do you treat people? What do you watch? Where do you go for comfort? Do you still "fast" or have you given up? Have you unconsciously resigned your faith and now you're just going via the motions?

I submit to you; please learn from Hannah's humility, I know I have.

God bless you,
Fwfm:nlw

Life Is Tough

Genesis 22

We've all had moments in life where we thought to ourselves; wow, life is tough. Whether it was a decision we were making or something that happened to us, we realize life is unpredictable and tough. It's that way for most of us and it was that way for many biblical witnesses also.

From Abraham to Joseph to Moses, to David to Paul, life was tough. Since we are studying Abraham let's concentrate on him. Abraham had to undergo the most stringent and intense trial we could imagine. Almost every day I think of what I would do when asked to sacrifice my child of promise after a childless marriage. What went through his mind to even contemplate this undertaking?

As you read the scriptures can you even imagine what was going through Abraham's head? As he looked up and saw the sacrificial spot in the distance, what was he thinking? It was said that his son Isaac must have been about sixteen or seventeen years old. After waiting all this time to have him due to his wife being barren now God wants to have him sacrificed?

Lord, I already left my homeland upon your request. I already waited until I was one hundred years old to have this child whom you told me was going to make me the father of many nations. Now you tell me to sacrifice him? Life is tough but this exceeds it all.

This is beyond faith and obedience. This has the appearance of cruel and unusual. I'm sure Satan must have whispered to Abraham; really Abraham, don't you think God has gone too far this time? Have you even thought about what your wife Sarah is going to say when you return home alone? Oh, the agony Abraham must have endured to be obedient unto God?

I'm sure all of these thoughts and more went through Abraham's head. Although a tough decision Abraham decided to go through with it. Abraham didn't second guess God, he had been with Him enough times to know when it was truly God speaking. Abraham didn't even find it necessary to question God; he just obeyed.

Was this unfair? Was it tough? Was it unreasonable? Of course it was! Mentally and emotionally this must have been eating Abraham up. He had already failed so many tests (Ishmael asking Sarai twice to play his sister). However, this test was extreme and it took a lot of faith. There was only one way for Abraham to show he believed God in this venture and that was through obedience.

What do we do when no one is looking? What do we do when God asks or tells us to do something? Do we obey or do we argue the point? Do we rationalize, justify, or excuse why we believe some other response is more appropriate? Do we know better than God?

It's obvious Abraham's servants and even his son Isaac had questions as the scriptures indicate. Abraham had wood and fire but no sacrifice. He then told his servants to wait while he and Isaac went forward. Hmm.

Where is the lamb dad? This took some real faith on Abraham's part. Life had now become tougher than it ever had been. When asked where the sacrifice is, Abraham tied that boy up and raised his knife saying "The Lord will provide."

As tough as life is God will always provide. Even in seemingly impossible situations. All the examples are in the Bible as witnesses. God knew we would run into tough situations in our lives over and over again. God had given us people like Abraham and Joseph to show how He provides. God said we would have trials and tribulations; "I have told you these things, so that in me you may have peace. In this world, you will have trouble. But take heart! I have overcome the world" (John 16:33).

We have to have faith like Abraham and Joseph. That faith will push us toward the will of God. There is always a blessing in the will of God. <u>That blessing</u> is for us and through us. We must not forfeit this blessing by fainting in tough times instead of trusting God.

It's always a special blessing and an amazing thing to watch what God will do when we yield to Him. Yes, life has hard trials but nothing is too hard for God.

God bless you,
Fwfm; nlw

In the Garden

Gardens are so beautiful. The Garden of Eden was lavish with so many varieties of trees and flowers. Nevertheless something was lurking in that garden that was not wholesome. Oh, it was pretty and it was colorful. It was great variety and a vision to behold. Somehow in our gardens weeds show up. Some of the weeds even have the nerve to produce flowers. Then here come the gophers and snails; you just can't have nice things without some type pest.

It doesn't even matter if we have a fence around our garden, somehow pest get in if no more than a neighborhood cat. So in theory the garden looks perfect. When we thought the garden out in theory it seemed perfect. Then reality set in. you see in this world in theory anything can look good; however, in practice you find out its true content. This happens with gardens and it happens with people.

As good as some folk look there are things that lurk inside of them that basically makes them poisonous. God tells us over and over again to look beyond what we can see but we get caught up in aesthetics. She looked good, he looked good, he sounded good, she had a nice figure; see there.

You know it's funny, God never promised us a life without troubles and trials or suffering. That's ideal but actually unrealistic. John 16:33 tell us that, "These things I have spoken to you, that in Me you may have peace. In the world you will have tribulation; but be of good cheer, I have overcome the world." God never promised us a rose garden. So please know there will be some pests in our garden, we must work through them.

God bless you,
Fwfm; nlw

Mountains and Valleys

I don't have to tell you life is not all mountaintop experiences. Every now and then and for some of us there will be some valleys. Let's talk about the mountains first, in fact let's talk about actual mountains since the Bible speaks of so many of them. How about Mt. Sinai; where Moses received the Ten Commandments from God? How about Mt. Moriah where Abraham offered Isaac as a sacrifice? Even Mt. Ararat where Noah's ark landed after the flood?

Jesus gave one of His most serious sermons on a mountain in fact it was called the Sermon on the Mount (Matt. 5:7). How about the Mount of Transfiguration (Mt. 17:1–8). Lastly, we certainly cannot forget Jesus told the disciples He would return on the Mount of Olives in Jerusalem (Matt. 24:25).

Mountain views take our breath away. I've stood on Mt. Wilson at Chantry Flats in Arcadia viewing all of Pasadena, Sierra Madre, and Arcadia—oh, what a sight. The vision is panoramic and beautiful. To be physically high like in an airplane or helicopter allows us to see what we normally cannot see. It's a good thing to have these mountaintop experiences but at some point we have to come down from the mountain.

It is the same thing spiritually; God allows us to see spiritual heights and it gives us direction and purpose. Many times it shapes our future. But we also need the valleys. We don't have to gorge them, they happen on their own. The valleys we see are not pretty like the Grand Canyon; they are crevices we fall into and have difficulty exiting. The valleys of life might be job loss, divorce, financial problems, illness, or a wayward child. Nevertheless God uses even these valleys to navigate our circumstances.

We must not give up in our valleys or foolishly think life is supposed to be all mountains. Valley experiences actually help us know God better. We also learn who we really are during our valley times. It is ironic how being in a low place or broken and helpless or even a dark time in our life can actually help us.

The Bible is replete with example after example of those going through valley experiences and becoming the better person for it. With God to help valleys can actually give us vision. Remember Jonah in the belly of a whale; he saw the light? That was certainly a valley experience.

Remember Job in all his woes; that was a serious valley. His own wife told him to curse God and die. After all Job went through physically, mentally and emotionally, through it all he saw God like he never saw him before (Job 42:5).

As we discuss mountains and valleys we talked about the Sermon on the Mount. This is where the Beatitudes were given. In this sermon it basically was Jesus telling us to go to the valley to get to the mountain (Mt. 5:3–12). Jesus wanted us to clearly see that true or real happiness is not always recognized.

All that glitters is not gold and all that appears bad may have plenty of good in it. We must keep in mind if God is not in wherever we are that alone should cue us it may not be real or wholesome. Life is not all a bowl of strawberries with whip cream on top. The world is not all butterflies and rainbows. Sometimes good can still come from the valleys of life.

Trials, bereavement, suffering, and loss of relationships can be serious moments of growth. The Beatitudes invited us to embrace what the world sees as negative. The spirit of mourning, hungering and thirsting, also being misused and slandered like Jesus and ultimately persecuted are all valleys. Nevertheless they are valleys that can help us depending on how we perceive them.

It's not so much the mountains or the valleys that is the issue as much what happens on the mountain or in the valley. Have we met God on the mountain? Did we take advantage of that time on top of the mountain to praise, honor, worship, and thank God?

Did we only see the valley as a place of difficulty or also as a place of refuge? No matter where we find ourselves the main thing is did we see God? Were our eyes opened to new truth and the glory of God?

God bless you,
Fwfm; nlw

Child's Play

> Then He said to me, "Son of man, have you seen what
> the elders of the house of Israel do in the dark, every
> man in the room of his idols? For they say, 'The Lord
> does not see us, the Lord has forsaken the land.'"
>
> —Ezekiel 8:12

It was always funny how kids playing hide and seek thought in their minds that as long as their eyes are covered you could not see them. Is it naive, yes, but they really believe it works and we've all played this game. That's fine for children because they don't know any better, but what about adults?

How do adults do something they know full well is wrong and yet justify it, rationalize it, or excuse it as if it did not happen or they had a good reason to do it? In other words we know what God said, but our case is special; it's different. Are we actually saying to God, he doesn't understand us and our situation? So His omniscience is suddenly not working?

God gave the prophet Ezekiel a vision of this very thing discussing being exiled in Babylon. Just because they did something in the darkness or some hidden land did they really think God could not see them or didn't care what they were doing?

This same concept is happening in society as we are approving any and everything. It's happening in schools as there are no more rules for good. Heck to please people we have even changed the spelling on many words so you could spell it however you please. Words like *donut/doughnut* or *ketchup/catsup*.

When it comes to sex just pick who you want to be with no matter what sex they are, the world says it doesn't matter. This is prevalent even in the church. Does it bring confusion for children, yes? It even brings confusion for adults. Is God happy? NO! Do we think God does not see us or doesn't care about the rules anymore?

No God has not missed what we are doing and He tells us, "14 If my people, which are called by my name, shall humble themselves, and pray, and seek my face, and turn from their wicked ways; then will I hear from heaven, and will forgive their sin, and will heal their land" (2 Chron. 7:14).

Yes, we are born in sin and shaped iniquity; in us that is in our flesh dwelleth no good thing according to the Word. This is why God is saying to us in Ezekiel 36:26: "26 A new heart also will I give you, and a new spirit will I put within you: and I will take away the stony heart out of your flesh, and I will give you a heart of flesh."

God is showing us grace and mercy despite our intentional sin and rebellion. This is the reason He sent His only begotten Son to save us. We have to accept Him and the Word for not just our salvation from sin but even our salvation from the effects of the world, the flesh and the devil. God wants to give us a new beginning but we have to accept it and not look back like Lot's wife.

God wants us to look forward, to grow up and not be a child anymore in our thoughts or in our heart. We cannot hide from God in any way.

> 7 Where can I go from Your Spirit?
> Or where can I flee from Your presence?
> 8 If I ascend into heaven, You are there;
> If I make my bed in hell, behold, You are there.
> 9 If I take the wings of the morning,
> And dwell in the uttermost parts of the sea,
> 10 Even there Your hand shall lead me.
> And Your right hand shall hold me.
> 11 If I say, "Surely the darkness shall fall on me,"
> Even the night shall be light about me;
> 12 Indeed, the darkness [ ]shall not hide from You,
> But the night shines as the day;

The darkness and the light are both alike to You.
(Psalms 139:7–12)

It would be good if you read the entire 139 Psalms as God knows us quite well because He made us. In knowing our condition God sought us out to save us from ourselves. What a love to save a person even when they are your enemy.

[8] But God demonstrates His own love toward us, in that while we were still sinners, Christ died for us. [9] Much more then, having now been justified by His blood, we shall be saved from wrath through Him. [10] For it when we were enemies we were reconciled to God through the death of His Son, much more, having been reconciled, we shall be saved by His life. (Rom. 5:8–10)

Let's get away from child's play and grow up in Christ.

God bless you,
Fwfm; nlw

Bitter and Sweet

Many times hurt just seems to hurt but there is healing is some hurt. Sometimes hurt helps us. We must pray, Father help me to see your goodness even in my times of trouble. The Psalmist saw this which is why he said in Psalms 119:65–72:

> 65 You have done many good things for me,
> O Lord, according to Your word.
> 66 "Teach me good judgment and knowledge,
> For I believe Your commandments.
> 67 Before I was afflicted I went astray,
> But now I keep Your word.
> 68 You are good, and do what is good;
> Teach me Your statutes.
> 69 "The proud have forged a lie against me,
> But I will keep Your precepts with my whole heart.
> 70 Their heart is as fat as grease,
> But I delight in Your law.
> 71 It is good for me that I have been afflicted,
> That I may learn Your statutes.
> 72 The law of Your mouth is better to me
> Than thousands of coins of gold and silver.

Embrace your pain and submit it to God. Ask Him to make your bitterness sweet and help you to garner what you can learn from it. Basically what you are doing here is longing to be transformed by the riches of God's truth.

In hard times, we can still find joy and hope. Many times even when our troubles may be caused by our own hand we can still trust in God's grace and mercy (look at v. 68). God is asking us to pursue him at all times even times of sorrow that we may feel His love and care. God will sometimes allow things to happen to us for us. Trust Him and seek Him no matter what you are going through.

Sleeping at the Wrong Time

You know there is a time to sleep and there is a time to wake up. Some of us sleep too much at the wrong time. There are a lot of things going on in our world that need our attention (prayers). Revelations 3:2 says, "2 Be watchful, and strengthen the things which remain, that are ready to die, for I have not found your works all that great before God." We are in the midst of a decaying world with the so-called Christians consenting to it all and voting for it. Meanwhile we are not even praying that God's will be done. I assure you God is not happy.

God does not care which political party we belong to but He does care about His Word. We should never think our world is so far gone we should just give up; that is not what God calls us to do. Spiritual fatigue is not pretty, it's sickening. Have we failed to notice the lethargy that has crept into our churches and our marriages and family and friends' relationship? Nobody gives a darn anymore, we just give up.

Jesus said what you have received and heard, hold it fast. What happened to that, we have just let go and given up; you can always pray for God's will, it shows concern. First check the man/woman in the mirror then pray that God's will be done. It's not your job to fix the world and anybody else but it is your job to pray for your world that meaning other people. This is not time to sleep as if you just don't care.

Jesus said to watch and pray (Matt. 26:41). First Peter 5:8, 9 said, "8 Be sober, be vigilant; because your adversary the devil, as a roaring lion, walketh about, seeking whom he may devour:

"9 Whom resist stedfast in the faith, knowing that the same afflictions are accomplished in your brethren that are in the world."

Paul said, "11 Put on the whole armour of God, that ye may be able to stand against the wiles of the devil.

"12 For we wrestle not against flesh and blood, but against principalities, against powers, against the rulers of the darkness of this world, against spiritual wickedness in high places.

"13 Wherefore take unto you the whole armour of God, that ye may be able to withstand in the evil day, and having done all, to stand." (Eph. 6:11–13)

Do you even see what we're up against; this is no time to sleep.

> 11 And that, knowing the time, that now it is high time to awake out of sleep: for now is our salvation nearer than when we believed.
>
> 12 The night is far spent, the day is at hand: let us therefore cast off the works of darkness, and let us put on the armour of light.
>
> 13 Let us walk honestly, as in the day; not in rioting and drunkenness, not in chambering and wantonness, not in strife and envying.
>
> 14 But put ye on the Lord Jesus Christ, and make not provision for the flesh, to fulfill the lusts thereof. (Rom. 13:11–15)

Wake up and please read the thirty-seven Psalms, it's forty verses, and too long to print; Google it. God bless you, Fwfm; nlw.

I'm Weighed Down, Lord...

Many times anxiety can get the best of us whether we want it to or not. We think we got it all down pat then apprehension and a certain uneasiness pops up. Agitation angst and misgiving follow right behind it. We become nervous and have this tension and we can't pinpoint it. Our spirit just won't be quieted and we have this pent-up anxiety.

Perhaps you don't want to admit it but something is burdening you down. You can't carry everything on your own shoulders. Perhaps it's time to admit you have a problem and take that burden to the Lord. Burdens don't go away on their own; they usually get heavier if not dealt with.

Oh, you can play semantics and call them concerns if you want; well, you sure are concerned a lot or you definitely have some great concerns. You know our Savior and Lord was tempted in all points like us and yet without sin. They sent Jesus through the ringer. One of his own disciples right under him deceived him and betrayed him (Judas). Another disciple denied him (Peter).

Jesus was poor or financially strained despite what the joy boy televangelists say, Jesus had meager resources. The Pharisees constantly chided Jesus because they were jealous he was helping people via counsel and healing. Heck, He even fed them when they were hungry.

Jesus had enough humility to know when to admit he needed His Father. He would go away and pray knowing what he was dealing with was going to take much more than his strength. It's ironic how Jesus knew that and responded appropriately, yet we deny we even need help.

Because of what Jesus went through He is always there for us making intercession on our behalf (Heb. 7:25). We must stop being so hardheaded and stubborn and allow God to take our burdens and trust Him to help us in our time of need. The Word says in 1 Peter 5:7: "⁷Casting all your care upon him; for he careth for you. Either you believe this or you don't."

The other thing to do when emotionally distressed is realize what Jesus did in his time of need and do likewise. Jesus trusted his Father while under great anguish. He went and prayed knowing the answer to his prayer was in his Father.

> ⁴¹ And he was withdrawn from them about a stone's cast, and kneeled down, and prayed,
> ⁴² Saying, Father, if thou be willing, remove this cup from me: nevertheless not my will, but thine, be done.
> ⁴³ And there appeared an angel unto him from heaven, strengthening him.
> ⁴⁴ And being in an agony he prayed more earnestly: and his sweat was as it were great drops of blood failing down to the ground.

Did you copy that, Jesus said not my will but thy will be done. Do you think he wanted to be beaten and put on a cross for something he didn't even do? Not only was it painful and hurt Jesus heart and body; he gave his life that we might have life. So yes, Jesus sympathizes with our weaknesses, hurts and pains. And yes, He intercedes on our behalf.

So the next time you are weighed down, do this:

> If the world from you withholds of its silver and
> its gold,
> And you have to get along with meager fare,
> Just remember, in His Word, how He feeds the
> little bird;
> Take your burden to the Lord, leave it there.

[Chorus:]
Leave it there, leave it there,
Just take your burden to the Lord oh and leave
it there.
If you trust him through your doubt, He will
surely bring you out.
Take your burden to the Lord, leave it there.

Now if your body suffers pain and your health
you can't regain,
And your soul is slowly sinking in despair,
Jesus knows the pain you feel, He can save and
He can heal;
Take your burden to the Lord, leave it there.

God bless you,
Fwfm; nlw

I'm Feeling Blue

This world has a way of knocking us down or bursting our bubbles. When this happens too often it can cause major frustration, anxiety, and depression. Of course there are multiple ways to combat this inescapable phenomenon. I will list a few so we can keep our heads above water.

1. We have to surrender all to God. He has told us to come to Him on numerous occasions to find peace and rest; we need to take Him up on this. We must stop trying to control everything in our life and surrender it to Him. If we refuse we are going to wear ourselves out because it's just too much for us to handle alone.

2. Once we give it to Jesus, leave it with Jesus; no trading back. We don't need to help him; He knows what he is doing. We don't need to interfere like we already have the answer. Either we believe God has the power or not.

3. Speaking of which, if we believe Jesus is the answer then we need to trust him. Here are a few scriptures to help us.

    A. "Cast your burden on the Lord, and He shall sustain you; He shall never permit the righteous to be moved." (55:22)

    B. "Come to Me, all you who labor and are heavy laden, and I will give you rest. Take My yoke upon you and learn from Me, for I am gentle and lowly in heart, and you will find rest for your souls. For My yoke is easy and My burden is light." (Matthew 11:28–30)

C. "Therefore humble yourselves under the mighty hand of God, that He may exalt you in due time, casting all your care upon Him, for He cares for you." (1 Peter 5:6, 7)

D. "Fear not, for I am with you; be not dismayed, for I am your God. I will strengthen you, yes, I will help you, I will uphold you with My righteous right hand." (Isaiah 41:10)

E. "²When thou passest through the waters, I will be with thee; and through the rivers, they shall not overflow thee: when thou walkest through the fire, thou shalt not be burned; neither shall the flame kindle upon thee."

4. So as you can see there are numerous scriptures in the Word of God to sustain us and give us peace and comfort; we just have to keep referring to them. Yes we will be challenged and have much discomfort but there is a way of escape even if only temporarily until the next assault.

5. Another way to stay strong while feeling blue is to praise God like David did when being chased by Saul. Constant praise of God encourages your soul because it reminds you of what God has already done for you and others. Look at no. 6.

6. "God is our refuge and strength, an ever-present help in trouble" (Psalm 46:1–3). "The name of the Lord is a strong tower; the righteous run into it and are safe" (Proverbs 18:10). "Do not grieve, for the joy of the Lord is your strength" (Nehemiah 8:10).

7. In no. 4, I mentioned being sustained by God; let me say this. Talking with the Lord may not seem as urgent as so many other things we get into but in actuality it is far more important. God didn't say we ought to thirst after righteousness for nothing. The more we meditate on His Word and praise Him the stronger we become. We gain knowledge, insight, discernment, and so many other things necessary to make it in this world.

8. My dear friends, I beseech you, if you want to get rid of your blues lean heavily upon the things I'm saying here. The impact will be immediate.

9. Do not, I repeat, do not concentrate on your circumstances. God is bigger than your circumstances. Whatever conflicts or misunderstandings you may be involved in surrender them to God. Our situation and circumstances change all the time but our God is constant. All of our worries and fears need to be surrendered to Him.

10. Please know every trial we face no matter how serious God's peace is available. The question is not what happens to us but how we respond to it. Will we let our feelings take us out into left field emotionally or will we swing spiritually based on the Word of God and all His promises?

11. God knows what we are going through and says in 1 Corinthians 10:13, "13 No temptation has overtaken you except what is common to mankind. And God is faithful; he will not let you be tempted beyond what you can bear. But when you are tempted; he will also provide a way out so that you can endure it."

12. Please be reminded God wants to give us peace in the midst of our turmoil; He wants to give us an inner quietness in this noisy, confused world. If we do it God's way His Word will interpret our problems and not our feelings. We must yield to the Holy Spirit to find our rest no matter what our circumstances.

13. We will need to humble ourselves and lose our pride. Accept the fact that God's way works. We are weak but God is strong and He will come through as always. Let your weakness bring you through to a place of humility so that God may show you once again He is all-powerful. Nothing is too simple, too silly, or too small for Him to handle.

God bless you,
Fwfm; nlw

Take Me Back

It's so common to start off in Christ so excited, so full of joy; we call that baby Christians. Then comes teenage Christian problems; misunderstandings, discouragement, and depression. Finally adult Christians, who are smacked with some of everything over and over again. Many times it is so difficult it causes them to revisit where they first met Christ. Yes, they revert, or backslide. Hence, the songwriter wrote the song "Take Me Back."

> Take me back, take me back dear Lord
> to the place where I first received you.
> Take me back, take me back dear Lord where I
> first believed.
>
> I feel that I'm so far from you Lord
> But still I hear you calling me
> Those simple things that I once knew,
> Their memories keep drawing me.
>
> I must confess, Lord I've been blessed
> But yet my soul's not satisfied.
> Renew my faith, restore my joy
> and dry my weeping eyes.
>
> I tried so hard
> to make it all alone
> I need your help
> Just to make it home.

Take me back, take me back dear Lord
to the place where I first received you.
Take me back, take me back dear Lord where I
first believed.

Well, in our learning more about Abraham we find he is no different. Abraham was called from a pagan land then sent to Canaan which was promised to him. He completely walked away from his old life as instructed by God. So did this end the story; no, it was just the beginning as it is with us?

Becoming a new Christian is not a finished project but actually a new birth. It's now that the struggle begins. We commit ourselves to Jesus, learn His Word, and receive power of the Holy Spirit. We literally grow up conquering old habits and sins. We learn how to forgive those who have severely wronged us, oh what bliss.

Then one day those old habits come a calling. "Remember when?" Problems and sins we thought we were past and thought we had conquered crop up; God help us. It's like Paul said in Romans 7:15–25:

> [15] I do not understand what I do. For what I want to do I do not do, but what I hate I do. [16] And if I do what I do not want to do, I agree that the law is good. [17] As it is, it is no longer I myself who do it, but it is sin living in me. [18] For I know that good itself does not dwell in me, that is, in my sinful nature.* For I have the desire to do what is good, but I cannot carry it out.
> [19] For I do not do the good I want to do, but the evil I do not want to do—this I keep on doing. [20] Now if I do what I do not want to do, it is no longer I who do it, but it is sin living in me that does it.
> [21] So I find this law at work: Although I want to do good, evil is right there with me. [22] For in my inner being I delight in God's law; [23] but I see

another law at work in me, waging war against the law of my mind and making me a prisoner of the law of sin at work within me. ²⁴ What a wretched man I am! Who will rescue me from this body that is subject to death? ²⁵ Thanks be to God, who delivers me through Jesus Christ our Lord!

Does any of this sound familiar; you might want to check The Living Bible or The Message, to make it even plainer. What a struggle, what a fight, old habits once conquered now return with a vengeance. It's like a war going on inside of us. What's that old saying, "You can take a man out of the country, but you can't take the country out of the man." Well, replace country with sin.

What happened to all that joy we felt and all those songs we sang? It's nothing but a struggle now; where is God? We are discouraged by others sin who look like they are getting away with it (they are not, and it's none of our business). Our flesh just won't die, it's like Jason in Halloween; die flesh, dog gone it.

Now our growth is stunted and we are spiritually paralyzed. This is Abraham's life. In Genesis 20, Abraham tells a big old lie and also has Sarah to join him in it. They told the king Abimelech that Sarah was Abraham's sister. The king therefore took her and was about to have his way with her when God interrupted him.

God struck Abimelech with some type disease which actually was a form of mercy. God told the king that Sarah was a married woman and he and Abraham needed to straighten this lie out, fix it right now. Had Abimelech touched Sarah, death would have struck him. We must understand sometimes when things happen to us it is actually God's mercy redirecting us. Mishaps in our lives sometimes keep us from something far worse. How God prevents us is often strange but effective.

Whatever Abraham's reasoning was for concocting so great a lie and having his wife to join in is immaterial. This was stuff old Abraham used to do. Sometimes such as in another Christian song, "Come Thou Fount of Every Blessing." We have to realize we are prone to wander and prone to leave the God we love. For whatever reason we return to our old foolishness like a pig returns to the slop or mud; we have to pray to God to seal us with His love and care. Were it not for God sealing us we would all wander off.

Oh, to grace how great a debtor daily I'm constrained to be, let that goodness like a fetter bind my wandering heart to Thee. Prone to wander, Lord, I feel it Prone to leave the God I love. Here's my heart, oh, take and seal it, seal it for Thy courts above.

God bless you,
Fwfm; nlw

Choices Matter

Genesis 19

No more interceding for Abraham. The angels have been dispatched. God left and Abraham returned to his tent, time for action. The angels came to Sodom in the evening hour. They dressed as ordinary men so they had no angelic appearance. The first person they meet is Mayor Lot, Abraham's nephew. Here is Mayor Lot in the city of Sodom and soon we will see how much of Sodom is in Lot.

Verses 1–3: In case you are wondering how we knew Lot was Mayor of the city, the scripture indicates it. Lot was sitting in the gateway greeting people and not just for hospitality; it was Lot's job. He officially welcomed people and checked out strangers to determine their purpose or business in coming to Sodom.

Now don't forget Lot chose to settle in Sodom because it was so beautiful while Abraham chose to settle outside Sodom. Genesis 13:12 said Lot went from being near Sodom to in Sodom and he was now an official in Sodom. He made his choice. Lot said it reminded him of the garden of the city of Egypt (13:10).

While Abraham learned about Egypt and chose God over it, Lot chose the plush land and location over God. Lot wanted it all; he wanted God and the world. Somehow Lot thought "the plains" was where he could make this magic happen. All the luxuries and culture of the pagans or godless but he would still worship God. Sounds like an oxymoron doesn't it? I'm going to be around wrong but in my heart I'm going to do right.

So 13:11 tells us Lot chose for himself "the plains." He didn't even respect his older wiser uncle Abraham. Lot made a conscious, calculated, selfish and ambitious choice. He lived in the plains, became known and wealthy, then actually moved into Sodom itself. He was part of the Sodomite society; a leader, yet still claiming to know and love God.

I suppose Lot hadn't read you can't serve two masters; you have to choose between God and the world. The ironic thing is the lack of a choice also matters. You see if you do not choose God you automatically choose the world by default. It is like pleading the fifth in court. Why can't you just answer the question and tell the truth?

The answer is simple for Lot, his concern was getting rich, getting power and influence, and getting fame. Lot did that too—oh, he did it quite well. What Lot also did was lose sight of what was really important. That was a close relationship with God and sharing God with others starting with his own family.

Now please understand Lot's move to the dark side was gradual. In fact it was so gradual I'm not sure Lot even knew he had backslid. Don't forget this started with Lot outside the city in "the plains." Lot later moved into the city. So we could say Lot was near it but not in it. Lot was close to it and took advantage of what Sodom had to offer but later decided to join in it.

I used to tell a story about the 3800 Block as I used to live in the 3600 Block of Lynwood. There were always wild parties in the 3800 Block. You could only see shadows and all the cars from the 3600 Block. One of my neighbors used to talk about how awful the people were until one day he decided to get a closer look.

What he found in the 3700 block was a full view of scantily clad women and loud music with lascivious suggestions. It would seem like this was close enough, but no, he had to go further as if he could not already see what it was all about. The neighbor went on down to 3750, then 3760, and so on until finally he was at 3800.

Oh, the sites, the women, they grabbed him saying, "Come on in here, baby, you know you want to dance" and dance he did. This neighbor was later asked about how bad it was at the 3800 block and he literally said, "Oh, it's not bad at all, in fact I'm going down there all the time now to the parties; it's fun. I guess he progressively changed his thoughts of the people due to now being one of them.

So what we have here is very distinct progression in Lot's choices. Lot ultimately became an official in the city. Lot who once was a clear follower of God has now compromised himself so he could gain prominence in Sodom. We could say in Lot's defense that he meant to do right, but somehow it didn't materialize. I'm sure lot figured he could influence the people of Sodom to receive the Lord. He could change their whole thought process thereby changing their society.

Of course Lot would have had to fight through the very deep culture. The folk were locked into husband/wife swapping, sex with anybody and everybody, this was their way. Sodom was mean, it didn't care about the poor, let them starve to death. Sodom was all about the big dog biting and stomping on the little dog.

It was kind of like today with all our strip clubs and gay bars and political views of let the homeless fend for themselves. Lot thought he could change this culture. He was going to have moral influence on this great city. Unfortunately as is so common or usual in situations like this, the city was a little more resilient then Lot expected.

Not only so, but Sodom loved its position; they were enjoying themselves. They felt like, who was this outsider to tell them how to live?

So unfortunately, Lot did not win any converts. He may have believed he was a witness of God but it didn't pan out. Lot was ignored by the inhabitants of the city. Sadly I would venture to say there may have been more of Sodom influence in Lot than Lot influence in Sodom. Lot caught Sodom's "disease," me first. Lot's motives were tainted and his worldly ambitions affected his alleged witness or testimony for God.

Probably something Lot had to resolve was did he weigh his success over his relationship with God. I mean come on, let's be honest here. How is your daily fellowship with God lot while you're at "Magic City." Just how many people have you convinced to follow God and walk away from evil?

Lot has your so-called riches that you obtained in Sodom really helped your life? Oh, one more important question Lot, let's say no one else is listening to you; but how is your family that you actually live with? Is your family following God or Sodom?

I've known people who literally choose churches based on the singing and people they can garner as friends. Despite poor teaching and poor preaching, they will remain at this church saying, no church is perfect. They will lose their kids to immorality, gangs, drugs or alcohol, but they stay with this church.

Why no Sunday school influence? What happened to Bible Training Union and Teen Outreach? Did you have Children's Church? So you mean to tell me nothing at this church helped your family and yet you stayed there—wow?

I think these are legitimate questions we have asked and more than reasonable comments and observations. Let's check the scripture and ascertain what Lots response is to the inquiries.

Verses 4–9: Lot I saw where you offered your alleged daughters as a proxy. How could you do that? What happened to you? Verses 6–8: There appears to be some serious debauchery and depravity going on, do you see that Lot?

Verses 4–11: In looking at the scripture we clearly see the makeup of the city. These are some degenerate folk. So these acts of sodomy (hence the name) were so common the city just adopted and accepted it. It was so prevalent until strangers were attacked and sexually assaulted by the same sex in the city square (mall). Now you're the mayor right Lot you can't clean this up?

We know you don't approve of this horrible behavior do you Lot? Second Peter answers for Lot in 2:7b–8. "[7] And delivered just Lot, vexed with the filthy conversation of the wicked:

"[8] (For that righteous man dwelling among them, in seeing and hearing, vexed his righteous soul from day to day with their unlawful deeds)."

So this did bother Lot yet he remained in Sodom? He made the choice to stay in a place that was beyond wicked. So the love of God or for God was less than Lots love for fame and fortune? What happened to you, Lot? You can have this whole world but give me Jesus, you hadn't heard that yet, huh? No, I chose prosperity first and somewhere down the line I attempted to fit God in.

So then, what would an honest answer from Lot be in his current relationship with God? If I'm honest, I would venture to say my relationship with God has been strained or blocked or obstructed or intercepted by numerous obstacles like wickedness in this great city of Sodom.

Okay, Lot, that appeared to be an honest answer though certainly not a refreshing enlightenment. Now Lot you stayed in a location with young daughters that was obviously blatantly ungodly to put it mildly. What did you hope to gain? Did you have any influence on the people of the city? Did they change their lifestyle and accept God because of your testimony?

According to the scripture, the citizens of Sodom not only did not follow Lot, they didn't even listen to him; Mr. Civil judge or Mayor or not. These people didn't respect or obey the law so why should they listen to Lot? This immoral character is who they were before Lot's arrival. Who was he, a stranger, to tell them how to live their lives? So did they hear you out Lot? NO!

Verses 9–11: It's getting pretty intense, some serious action is about to occur. No more playoffs, semi-finals and such, we are in the final stretch now. Even Lot's own family was not listening to him. His son-in-laws to be considered Lot's testimony a joke; they never took him seriously (12–14).

So now Lot can not only not reach the community he can't even reach his family (but wait for it; it's gets worse).

Abraham knew Lot was in this city with his family but remember he stayed out and prayed that at least fifty righteous down to ten righteous be saved. I guess Abraham was hopeful Lot had some influence, but it just wasn't so. Lot's own son-in-laws to be who were engaged to his daughters didn't believe a word Lot said about God.

Not only so but apparently they were just like the rest of the men in the city and "active with whomever" as we shall later see. Something about Sodom and these fiances rubbed off on Lot's daughters (wait for it).

Lot, another thing I want to ask; what did you get out of this whole venture? I know you were looking for wealth and power, how did that work out? What do you have to show for the time you spent in this wicked place? You were looking for the next great thing; did you find it?

Verses 15–17

The angels told Lot you need to leave here NOW! Get your wife and daughters and go and DO NOT look back. There is nothing to look at or look for back there, GET OUT!

Go on now, get out of "the plains" unless you want the same thing these folk are going to get. It was as if Lot wanted to do right but just had no intestinal fortitude to do so. He chose wrong (v. 18–20).

Verse 23: It rained fire and brimstone on Sodom and Gomorrah. So all that remained of everything Lot invested in was black charred ground. But it gets worse, Lot's wife decided to take one last look at her birth place and all she loved.

Yes, the angels specifically told her to leave and not look back. In disobeying this advice she turned to a pillar of salt. Wow!

Now Lot has lost all his material gain and his wife. Mrs. Lot felt she left something back in Sodom and in turning to look for it she was done (but it gets even worse) (vv. 30–36).

This is really bad so you may have to send the kids to another room now. Lot's two daughters apparently were exposed to some vile stuff. These girls claim they were virgins but apparently they were perverted at least in their minds. They thought of a degenerate and depraved plan because they had become spiritually corrupted.

Before you go on please read the text so you can be prepared for what is about to come; the shock is incredible. These young women got their father drunk so they could sleep with him just to have a child. Yep, where did that come from? (Sodom). They succeeded (v. 36).

The children of these girls grew into nations that fought with Israel (Moabites and Ammonites). You see what bad choices can do? They can reverberate like a rock hitting water and causing waves.

Now Lot has nothing to look back on but wasted years in Sodom. He lost his wife; he is shamed and full of regret. Everything that was happening now was because he chose Sodom. We clearly see when one tries to get the best of both worlds you can't. Not only do you get hurt but others also suffer—sometimes to the fourth and fifth generations.

This is painful; this didn't have to happen. It was a poor choice from the beginning. Now everything is destroyed due to decisions that were not thought through. Choices matter!

God bless you,
Fwfm; nlw

How Does Prayer Work?

Genesis 18:16–33

Let's stay with the theme of the life of Abraham but let's talk about his prayers. What was he praying about? Why was he praying? What happened when he prayed?

Isn't it amazing how many cultures that were once strong and thriving who ceased to be? What happened? The lack of human concern and really poor morals happened. Also idolatry permeated the land. You can't help only the rich, kill the poor, have sex with anybody, and sacrifice people to the gods.

You might do that but after a while your whole society breaks down. You've got no spiritual infrastructure, no moral fiber and integrity and this is sorely needed to have a good foundation in society. It's like a body that slowly loses its legs. You cease to be as strong as you were. Combine that with other losses and you can severely handicap a whole city, state, and country.

Look at verses 16–21, dinner is over and God and the angels are about to leave. They looked down at "The Plains" (Sodom, Gomorrah, Admah, Zeboiim, Bela) (Gen. 14:3), because God was about to end this nonsense. It had become just too immoral.

Why did God reveal His intentions to Abraham? Because He knew what Abraham would say and he wanted to give him the opportunity to say it. So here is Abraham and his guest leaving dinner and heading toward Sodom. As they look down at the valley of the Dead Sea, they speak their thoughts.

Have you ever watched someone or something before it wrecks itself? They never saw it coming; everything was just fine to them. God speaks to the angels before they carry out their assignment and

He lets Abraham hear the conversation. From where they are standing, they all have a bird's eye-view. Soon it would be no more.

Now God could have kept this to himself but He chose to share it with Abraham; why? I'll tell you why; again because aside from wanting to give Abraham an opportunity to offer his opinion God was actually baiting Abraham to pray. Abraham didn't just start praying, God started Abraham to pray by what God said intentionally.

So what does this mean? It means many times God moves us to pray so He can answer it. He uses several forms of motivation. He speaks to us via the Spirit (Living Word). He speaks to us via the Bible (written Word). He speaks to us via the preacher (spoken Word).

He allows job loss, sickness, death, family problems, financial issues, and etc. Yes, many of the occurrences in our life are not caused by God, but they are allowed by God or permitted. They all have reason and purpose that is beyond our understanding.

Too many of us have ignored God like He is not talking to us so God has ways of getting our attention. Please keep in mind that prayer is not just us talking to God about what we want. Think about it; prayer is God prompting us to talk to Him about something to assist us in this life. It may be spiritual, emotional, mental, physical, or financial. Without God's prompting we would have neglected to ask for what God knew we needed. Wow!

God is not an ATM. God is not there just to bless our plans. God always goes above and beyond what we imagine to give us what we really need. Please don't give me that nonsense the "Joy Boys" (televangelist) come up with to extract money from you. Pray in faith. Come into agreement with God. Plant a seed and let God bless it. God gave me a revelation. You have to get in allegiance with God. God gave me a revelation. If any of this sounds familiar you should be very careful so you're not taken in by nonsense to empty your pockets.

You say how gullible can we be? Well, these joy boys ain't rich for nothing. They have somebody's money and they are millionaires. If you really want to pray a prayer of faith why don't you act on the

<u>Word of God</u>? Not as interpreted by the "Joy Boys" giving you joy sermons to make you feel good while you continue in sin.

Really look at the Word and ask God what is next; what would you have me do? If the answer is really from God it will line up with His Word, the Holy Spirit, and preaching. If even one is off it is suspect. God is always true to His Word.

So now back to Abraham, the friend of God according to James 2:23, 2 Chronicles 20:7, and Isaiah 41:8. Ah, so this is the reason God shared with Abraham His intention for "the Plains." Yes, Abraham was considered His friend. We don't keep "our friends" in the dark when something heavy is pending. I don't want to digress so let me go on because that is another whole sermon.

God called this man Abraham to be the father of many nations. God was miraculously bringing this about. Why not now reveal to His friend His plans? Did you know God is trying to do the same thing with us? God is trying to get our attention one way or another. Are you listening or does God have to permit destruction of "the plains" in your life?

God favors us and wants the best for us but that doesn't mean He just wants to give us "stuff" as the joy boys always say. God wants us to make good decisions that help us in every way especially spiritually and emotionally. He has already given us His Son and His grace. We currently live in the disposition of grace. Nothing we did per se put us where we are multiplying what He already gave us.

<u>We are strategically where we are as God has allowed</u> and <u>blessed.</u> God has plans for us but we must listen to Him. We must take our cue as we are prompted to pray. We must walk in obedience to God's will and not what we want When we ask for something is it what God wants or what we want? When we ask for something will it help just you or will it bless somebody else? I'll tell you this; God ain't telling His secrets to just anybody. He's telling them to His friends. Those who are obedient and listening to His will.

God has enlisted us as believers in His army. We are supposed to be ready for spiritual warfare and salvation of souls. We are loaded with weapons according to Ephesians 6:12–18. We are ambassadors for Christ according to 2 Corinthians 5:20. It ain't always about you. It may be for you but about others; God has a plan.

God takes care of His friends. Are you listening? God is not just enlisting anybody; this is a partnership. Obedience is big time in the service. You have to know how to follow directions and take orders.

Look at verses 18–21. Do you really think God needed to visit "the plains"? To ascertain what was happening. We know God already knew in His omniscience, but this is what He told Abraham. This was for Abraham's benefit to prompt him to pray. How bad had it gotten that God could hear this nonsense all the way to heaven? Well, let's look at it.

At the moment in "the plains" there was extreme violence, outright greed, deplorable despicable sexual depravity (kind of like it is now except we are worse). Kids and women were being sacrificed; it was pretty bad. Look at your TV today. Shootings at elementary schools, high schools, theaters, and churches yet the people don't want gun control and gun laws.

The internet is just out of control. Kids and adults are lured to La-La Land of immorality and they willingly go with eyes wide open. Some are never to be seen again. Pornography is in every form, including cartoons. You can now vape (smoke or inhale) flavors of tobacco. (Who do you think that is designed for?)

Auto theft video games have levels to get prostitutes in cars. The CEO said he didn't think anyone would reach those levels. Practically every video game made now has naked or partially clad girls with sex and killing; guns are prevalent. You cannot distinguish between Christian homes and worldly homes as the divorce rate is the same in both.

The dirty rotten preachers that people are supposed to respect and trust to help will not touch these subjects. They say they don't want to lose support telling people negative things. Now no families have been helped, no marriages have been saved, yet the people remain at these churches. There is no prayer meeting, no Bible study and no Sunday school; they are on the bulletin, but nobody comes and nobody emphasizes that they should.

There is a great outcry of human sin just like in biblical days; here we go again. Also just like biblical days it is the so-called good folk-Christians or lack thereof, they can't be found. These people of the plains have no concern for the poor and needy. They were arrogant and homosexuality was out of control. Men were raping other men (Ezek. 16:49–50).

The people of the plains considered themselves better than other people. They were gluttons for themselves but left the poor to die in the streets. God didn't matter to them; they were god. Lying, child abuse, murder and perversion of every sort was the order of the day and God had enough. Time to end it like in the days of Noah— no mass.

Well, Abraham watched as the two angels put a little gallop in their step toward "the plains." Abraham wasn't blind or deaf; he knew what was about to happen so he started to pray. Well I'll be. Abraham walked up to the Lord immediately and started praying (vs. 22–32).

Really, Abraham, you're asking about good people or righteous people in "the plains"? But God listens and responds because He already knows the answer. While we are on the subject of good people let me parenthetically add this. The Word says there is none righteous no not one (Eccles. 7:20, Ps. 14:3, and Rom. 3:20); so please understand we cannot laud over one another, we're all jacked up. If we haven't done one thing we have done something else. We are under the grace of God. You've no doubt heard the expression "but for the grace of God there go I"? That's real, how wonderful is God's grace and mercy.

So this is how prayer works. God prompted Abraham to pray. God then answered Abraham's prayer. Remember God answers are always yes, no, and not right now. Accept His answer; don't act like you didn't hear it because you don't like it.

Yes, we can appeal to God's mercy to go beyond His grace. God's answer may surprise even us. Of course the judge of all the earth will do right. Will God save some wicked folk in the process of trying to save some righteous? NO! The wicked will have every opportunity to accept God. When they refuse God will accept their answer and act accordingly (2 Pet. 3:8–10).

Remember, we all have sinned and come short of the glory of God. The only difference is righteous folk have accepted God's grace. Unrighteous folk figure I don't need God or His grace. Believe it or not it is only because of the righteous folk that God has not punished us just like Sodom and company.

We currently live in the dispensation of grace. We are preserving the World and trying to get as many as will receive the grace of God. This is the only thing keeping God from destroying us. The world is once again fully corrupt and it's not getting any better.

God's mercy is delayed until everyone has had an opportunity to make a decision for Christ. When you look at the text it's pretty clear Abraham knows there are not fifty righteous folks in all "the plains." Abraham is not presumptuous; he appeals to God with full respect for reality. So let me throw this in; when those "joy boys" start talking to devil while praying, "Satan, we command you…Bind him, Lord, Satan, we bind you in the name of Jesus." This prayer is full of dung.

Let's put things in perspective. With all of what we have done and those like us, who are we to order the prince of darkness around. Even Michael the ark angel didn't do that in Jude 9. Those prideful prayers to convince people we have power are nothing but empty words, not true prayers.

In fact, we ought to be careful messing with spirits of the darkness and wickedness in high places. The last man that did this according to Paul got in serious trouble, see Acts 19:12–17. Remember, there is nothing to us were it not for the Jesus in us.

God permits us to pray to Him and we have the lack of humility and the audacity to come at Him in pride. That is not how prayer works.

Let me ask you this: when you pray to God is anybody going to get something out of the answer other than you. You just might be praying amiss.

Back in our story, Abraham is praying for the lost; namely his nephew Lot who is stuck in "the plains." Have you ever wondered why Abraham stopped at praying for at least ten righteous? You think he knew only Lot and his wife and daughters and their fiances were righteous? That is even less than ten according to Genesis 19.

So you mean Mayor Lot (yes, he had become the mayor), had no influence over anyone else in the city? No Christian friends, acquaintances, associates, or such? No fellowships or dinner parties among the righteous? Nope, they were "busy" too. This sounds just like the so-called church today. (Okay, let's keep it moving.) But let me just say this, you mean even though Lot was the mayor for Sodom at this time his Christian witness or testimony bore no fruit? You haven't seen anything yet, just keep reading.

Abraham was well aware of this, which is why he chose to live elsewhere. The plains were like 849 Summit in Pasadena. As policemen, we made over fifty arrests a month at this location for robbery, grand theft auto, drug sales and use, and prostitution. This went on for multiple years. It was also well known to everyone so why would a person in their right mind choose to live there. Abraham said, "No way, no 849 Summit for me and my household" (Josh. 24:15).

The immortality and callous indifference of the people of the plain was incredible. It was beyond disgusting. In compassion, Abraham was praying to God for mercy for all the folk. If it is any way possible, Lord, please have mercy?

Now I want to say something you may have missed in reading the text. Look at 18:33 again. Did you see that? We see prayer as us talking to God, us conversing with God. Well, look how this turned out God was the last one talking. We believe we are talking to God when in fact God is talking to us. Abraham didn't start this prayer and neither did he finish it. God started it and God concluded it. So we could surmise that prayer is actually God talking to us.

Now "the Plains" were so bad even Lot's whole family didn't make it out. In Genesis 19, even the fiancés of the daughters of Lot said they couldn't go because they were leaving too much behind. Wow!

The angels specifically told Mrs. Lot, Lot and his daughters, "get out" and "don't look back." I feel like preaching now. In other words ain't nothing back there for you; that place is being destroyed.

Go on now, get out to safety. I'd like to work this more but I must go on.

God set the limits to this prayer or conversation. Then He sent the angels about their business. Paul expounded on this in Rom. 8:26b. We appreciate and acknowledge Abraham's heart of compassion and mercy that we should all possess.

Prayer is a partnership with God. What a joy to experience our friend, the creator of the world sharing with us His intentions. Wow! He doesn't need our help but He will hear us out then tell us how it's going to work. We can appeal to His mercy and sometimes in His permissive will he will alter the course. This is not that time.

"9 For we are co-workers in God's service; you are God's field, God's building." (1 Cor. 3:9)

"6 Be careful for nothing; but in every thing by prayer and supplication with thanksgiving let your requests be made known unto God." (Phil. 4:6)

Please hear me out on the whole point of prayer. As God's fellow workers will get something out of each prayer. Our circumstances may not change because we prayed but we will change. Yes, the problems may remain, the financial issues, the poor relationships, and/or divorce, even the major illness and etc.

So then, what is the point of prayer you ask, because something in us changes? We become a better person. (Oh, I wish I could preach here.)

When I prayed at Pasadena Police Department for twenty-three years absolutely nothing changed; in fact, it got worse. Well what happened preacher, how did you last that long. God changed me. Meanwhile I pastored seventeen families in the police department. I married supervisors and pastored their children. Oh, how I prayed to God to please deliver me from these evil people. I would so love to adlib here but I must go on.

Abraham never mentioned Lot by name but both He and God knew what and whom he was referring to. God answered that prayer by sending the angels to rescue Lot and his family. The city was going to be destroyed but God removed Lot and his family first due to Abraham's prayer.

Let me say to you as I said to myself over and over again. When things go all wrong, I mean seriously south and it's very dark to the point where you come to this conclusion. Well, that was a disastrous waste. Why didn't you answer my prayer, Lord? First of all, you don't know what God was planning via the whole episode. You are not entitled to know it all.

> [8] "For my thoughts are not your thoughts, nei-
> ther are your ways my ways," declares the Lord.
> [9] "As the heavens are higher than the earth, so are
> my ways higher than your ways and my thoughts
> than your thoughts." (Isa. 55:8, 9)

Even though God does share some things sometimes He is not obligated to do so. Just because things don't turn out like you expected it doesn't mean the answer didn't come. Prayer is about God, not about us.

God's plans can be altered via our prayers and His permissive will. It does not give us control of any sort, only a partnership in the plans of God. In most cases God has "fixed" times and dates in His eternal plans. No man knows the times and dates. God does leave room in His permissive will for some things like healing, relationships, and etc.

For example, Nineveh was as good as destroyed but due to prayers God stayed the judgment. He sent Jonah. Now Jonah who was a racist told God he didn't like the people and they didn't deserve to be saved. Jonah further told God he was not going to preach to them and ran away. If you don't know this story go read Jonah I must move on.

Another example is 2 Kings 20:1–11 when King Hezekiah was dying and he prayed. God extended his life for another 15 years. Prayer works, so pray, but leave the results to God.

God bless you,
Fwfm; nlw

Where Is God in My Pain?

When we go via adversity we can actually become a whole different person. It's is so easy when things are going well. Good job, good marriage, good kids, nice home, good friends; who's not happy? Now you lost your job and it put pressure on your marriage. Your sixteen-year-old daughter just got pregnant and you just discovered your seventeen-year-old son is gay. Is it getting interesting yet?

You lose your home to foreclosure then discover you may have cancer and you have no medical insurance. Do I have your attention? Now you've been going to church all your life but now you're suddenly not interested. Is it the church, is it the Word, or is it God who just seemingly doesn't seem to be working for you anymore?

So would that make you a fair weather Christian? As long as things were going well you could praise God but now that things are awry suddenly you just have no use for God? Wow! So what you're really asking is where is God in my pain?

How could God allow this to happen to me? I've always served Him. I've always went to church. I've always treated people with decency and respect. How could God let my family be attacked like this? This is so painful; where is God?

Please understand the world is which we live is mean, evil and uncaring. Everyone is more concerned about where they are and what they can get, even so-called family. When you get down and out not too many people are going to care. Now you want to dismiss God who really cares?

To answer your question where is God in my pain and how could He allow this to happen to me? When Adam and Eve ate of that fruit in Genesis it was the tree of knowledge of good and evil.

They ate us out of house and home. Our world may have plenty knowledge but it also has plenty of evil. Our pain is part of that evil.

Where is God you say, the same place He was when He sent Jesus Christ to the cross because of our sins and for our salvation? I like the way Isaiah 53 said it. I'm going to print only three verses but you should read the whole chapter.

> ³ He is despised and rejected of men; a man of sorrows, and acquainted with grief: and we hid as it were our faces from him; he was despised, and we esteemed him not.
> ⁴ Surely he hath borne our griefs, and carried our sorrows: yet we did esteem him stricken, smitten of God, and afflicted.
> ⁵ But he was wounded for our transgressions, he was bruised for our iniquities: the chastisement of our peace was upon him; and with his stripes we are healed.
> ⁶ All we like sheep have gone astray; we have turned every one to his own way; and the Lord hath laid on him the iniquity of us all.

Yes, it pained God to send His only Begotten Son to suffer and die for our sin but He did. God loved us just that much (John 3:16). Just think, if they did this to the green tree behold what shall they do to the dry? (Luke 23:31).

Romans 3:23 says, "23 For all have sinned and fall short of the glory of God." Paul goes further to say in Romans 6:23, "23 For the wages of sin is death, but the gift of God is eternal life in Christ Jesus our Lord."

As you go via your misery in life, broken home, broken marriage, broken heart, and broken life, then sickness and death strike like a snake, don't blame God and whatever you do don't leave God. Get closer to God. Look on Christ tear stained face and recognize how much He loved us. If you want to find God or Jesus in your pain, go to the cross.

The songwriter put it so well when he said,

Alas! and did my Savior bleed
And did my Sov'reign die?
Would He devote that sacred head
For such a worm as I?

At the cross, at the cross where I first saw the light
And the burden of my heart rolled away
It was there by faith I received my sight
And now I am happy all the day

Was it for crimes that I had done
He groaned upon the tree?
Amazing pity! grace unknown!
And love beyond degree!

Well might the sun in darkness hide
And shut his glories in
When Christ, the mighty Maker died
For man the creature's sin

But drops of grief can ne'er repay
The debt of love I owe
Here, Lord, I give myself away
'Tis all that I can do

God bless you,
Fwfm; nlw

Guess Who's Coming to Dinner?

Genesis 18:1–15

How many times have you spoken to someone who went to a church and had a problem with an usher? How many times have you talked with someone and they told you they went to a church for several years and nobody talked to them? These are common stories that have happened to a lot of people.

Here in Genesis 18, let's keep in mind Abraham has a new name now and a regenerated heart. Have you ever heard of Middle Eastern hospitality; well, it's real? Do you remember the Bible saying be careful entertaining because you may entertain angels unaware? That's real too.

Notice how the chapter starts by discussing the great trees of Mamre. You know this is the same place where Abraham was when he got word that his nephew Lot was taken prisoner by kings in the east (Gen. 14:3).

Here in our text today, three strangers show up out of the clear blue. One of them is the Lord himself. Verses 1–5: God with two angels show up and as we keep reading we find these are the same two angels who go to Sodom to save Lot and destroy the city.

We know from reading the text that Abraham did not recognize them; he had no clue who they were at this time. What God was doing here is testing whether or not Abraham had truly acquired a circumcised heart.

Getting back to earlier when I asked if any of you ever met a rude usher or a church that doesn't know its members. What if God sent angels to your church unawares? We have a tendency to help the well-dressed or Mercedes drivers but the old Fords and Chevys we disregard.

I personally have gone to too many churches where degrees in biblical studies were claimed. The question really is, what did the degrees have to do with being led by the Spirit of God? When you don't know someone and you are applying for job and the boss meets you in the lobby acting like just another applicant; now that's a test.

Impromptu emergencies, car accidents, sick friends, and divorced friends, that's a test. It is easy to claim regeneration and a circumcised heart when you have no troubles and trials. What about after you lose your job or lose a loved one? These are true rude awakenings; you find out just who people really are.

So here is Abraham now on a hot desert day meeting and greeting perfects strangers. Verses 6–8: Abraham quickly springs into action and tells Sarah to prepare food and drink for the strangers. Abraham didn't act alone but he got his wife and servants involved in showing the three guests hospitality.

I wonder, have we ever attempted to meet the needs of strangers or are we only concerned about impressing our pastor with our tithes and offerings? Do we give to disaster relief funds or people going via a tragedy in lieu of tithes and offering? Oh that's right we want that tax break credit so we have to make sure we give to an institution and not a person in need. So did we give it for the tax break or out of love?

You do realize we are the ambassadors of Christ we should therefore be sharing Christ love and kindness outside the walls of our church. You can help people you don't know. Perhaps the reason a lot of church folk can't grow is because they never seek relationships outside the church. They are only interested in the other so-called believers. What about Revelation 3:20?

Jesus sought to save whoever was lost not just certain folk. You can't save all the black and leave the White out. You can't save all the White and leave the Latino out. You can't save only the Latinos and leave the Asians out. Where is your circumcised heart? You ain't changed a bit. You received the love of Christ but it stopped at you.

NAUM WARE

It was designed to flow to you and through you; that is if your heart is circumcised.

The true test of our faith is do we love others as Christ loved us? Read Matthew 25:31–46. So many times I have preached this illustration in the previous text. I used to take the whole church to convalescent homes. Just remember folks when you don't help others in need it shows your true heart. You can claim to know Jesus all you want; your actions will give you away.

> [27]Pure religion and undefiled before God and the Father is this, To visit the fatherless and widows in their affliction, and to keep himself unspotted from the world. I keep telling people these especially so-called Christian politicians. We really need to be about our Father's business. (James 1:27)

Let's look back at Abraham now. He didn't help the strangers and offer them dinner to win brownie points. He wasn't trying to impress them. Abraham was being genuine in loving concern. He had no idea who these strangers were.

Verses 9–15: The men asked Abraham where his wife was. This is when he must have got his first clue these men were not normal. First of all how did they know her name when she had just got a new name from Sarai to Sarah? How did they even know he was married? I'm telling you, know when God is speaking to you. There was a message in this for Abraham and Sarah.

Sarah laughed to herself, not out loud yet the Lord knew she laughed and commented on it. In other words, listen you've already greatly erred with the Hagar stunt; are you saying this is too hard for God? Remember this same promise had been made years before? Now God gives them a time frame.

Sarah looked down at her ninety-year-old body and felt like, seriously? God read her mind or thoughts and called her out on it. She said, I didn't laugh. God said, "Yeah, you did!" Know whom you are dealing with. Now Sarah was scared realizing there is nothing we can hide from God. We are an open book (heart and mind).

This is why Romans 4:19–22 is so important.[19] And being not weak in faith, he considered not his own body now dead, when he was about an hundred years old, neither yet the deadness of Sarah's womb:

> [20] He staggered not at the promise of God through unbelief; but was strong in faith, giving glory to God;
> [21] And being fully persuaded that, what he had promised, he was able also to perform.
> [22] And therefore it was imputed to him for righteousness.

Can you imagine what must have happened once those three strangers left? Sarah was saying like, who was that? She caught on too this time. Paul speaks of this in Hebrews 11:11: [11]Through faith also Sarah herself received strength to conceive seed, and was delivered of a child when she was past age, because she judged him faithful who had promised.

Realization is big; it gives us the power to believe and receive. In Sarah's case, conceive. The angel told her, is anything too hard for God? Knowing God's faithfulness Sarah was now saying, okay let's roll. Let it be even as you have said. It's a beautiful thing when the character of the one promising is above reproach.

So when God says I can turn your darkness into light or I can give you peace in the midst of your storm you can believe Him. Nothing is impossible for our God. It's not about believing in us or our friends or even our circumstances. It's about believing and trusting in God. Our faith is in an unfailing God.

For those of you who have read the Bible many times over, one of the phrases that you see all the time is "fear not." The other is "but God." These are there for a reason. Not only is it in the Bible but it is in both the Old Testament and the New Testament. Angels telling man to "fear not," it meant God is about to do something unusual but don't let it scare you.

When it comes to "but God" it is talking about something that has already occurred and we thought it was final, "but God." For example, Genesis 31:42 (NIV): [42] In fact, except for the grace of God—the God of my grandfather Abraham, even the glorious God of Isaac, my father—you would have sent me off without a penny to my name. But God has seen your cruelty and my hard work, and that is why he appeared to you last night."

"20 You intended to harm me, but God intended it for good to accomplish what is now being done, the saving of many lives." (Gen. 50:20, NIV)

> [14] David stayed in the wilderness strongholds and in the hills of the Desert of Ziph. Day after day Saul searched for him, but God did not give David into his hands. (1 Sam. 23:14)

"My flesh and my heart may fail, but God is the strength of my heart and my portion forever." (Ps. 73:26)

> "[15] You killed the author of life, but God raised him from the dead. We are witnesses of this." (Acts 3:15)

I'm sure you missed the "but God" at first but you see how it mattered. It ain't over until God says so. The place to look is where man has given up and surrendered to hopelessness or thrown his hands up in despair. I like the way the songwriter said don't you dare give up, "Our God reigns."

> [23] They are new every morning: great is thy faithfulness.
> [24] The Lord is my portion, saith my soul; there-fore will I hope in him.
> [25] The Lord is good unto them that wait for him, to the soul that seeketh him.

[26] It is good that a man should both hope and quietly wait for the salvation of the Lord. (Lam. 3:23–26)

Remember folks God is not a man that He should lie. What He says He will fulfill. You just be ready when He comes to dinner.

God bless you,
Fwfm; nlw

Circumcision

Genesis 17 (read your Bible).

We all know what circumcision means. Here we find it's origination. God wanted to separate His people from the pagans or non-believers. What better way than to start with the male procreative organ. By removal of the foreskin it physically separated God's chosen people. This loose cap or tip represented fallen humanity. We were getting rid of sinful flesh inherited from the fall of Adam. It's a symbolic gesture yet it is a physical incision, a cutting away of sin.

Was this command of God strange, yes? Did it have a purpose, yes? This was Old Testament and once the New Testament came along Paul used the same terms except now instead of circumcising the male foreskin Paul speaks of circumcising the heart (Col. 2:11–13).

> [11] In him you were also circumcised with a circumcision not performed by human hands. Your whole self ruled by the flesh was put off when you were circumcised by Christ 12 having been buried with him in baptism, in which you were also raised with him through your faith in the working of God, who raised him from the dead. 13 When you were dead in your sins and in the uncircumcision of your flesh, God made you alive with Christ. He forgave us all our sins.

Remember the New Testament is simply a fulfilling of the Old Testament. The topic here is a circumcised heart. This circumcision is done by the Spirit of the Lord. God is helping us to choose properly or assisting us to choose. In Old Testament a cutting away of flesh; in the New Testament it was a change of mind and heart such as in 2 Corinthians 5:17: [17] Therefore if any man be in Christ, he is a new creature: old things are passed away; behold, all things are become new.

God reminds us again and again we cannot serve two masters. We cannot serve self and God at the same time. God will not accept divided loyalty. God wants the old flesh cut away. He wants a complete change of heart, mind, and soul.

This can only occur when we give Jesus lordship over our lives. We cannot just say we know Him we have to accept Him over whatever we had before and follow him.

> [24] Then Jesus told his disciples, "If anyone would
> come after me, let him deny himself and take up
> his cross and follow me. (Matt. 16:24)

Every area of our life must change. We all have hidden sins and habits that we justify, excuse, and rationalize. These must be purged. We must want them to go via the executive powers of our will. We must fully surrender as a suspect with his hands up and being apprehended. Search me, Lord, and take me, I am no longer running away.

May the lamp of God shine into our life exposing everything and burning up the dross? Everything that binds us to the world must go.

Verses 3–5, 15–16: God is so serious about this until He even changes Abram's name to Abraham. Abram meant "exalted father." We're past that now; you are now "father of nations." Oh, by the way, I'm changing Sarai's name too. Sarai means "contentious" or quarreler, we know that's true of Sarai. She now shall be called Sarah.

"Gentle and quiet spirit," Sarah shall be full of grace and obedience and godly womanhood. Certainly looks like a lot of us could use a name change.

God didn't want just a sign in the flesh but in the heart and mind. The heart is the symbol of the soul. It is the seat of the mind, emotions, and will. The mind and will are our executive faculties; they make the decisions for us. They are our foundation and seat of strength. So if our foundation is cracked or warped that would mean anything standing on top of it is jeopardized.

When our heart is right, we do right. This is why God wants our heart circumcised.

> "3 For we are the circumcision, which worship God in the spirit, and rejoice in Christ Jesus, and have no confidence in the flesh." (Phil. 3:3)
> "5 Casting down imaginations, and every high thing that exalteth itself against the knowledge of God, and bringing into captivity every thought to the obedience of Christ." (2 Cor. 10:5)
> "14 But put ye on the Lord Jesus Christ, and make not provision for the flesh, to fulfil the lusts thereof." (Rom. 13:14)

I'm trying to help someone here but you have to follow the instructions of God's Word.

God bless you,
Fwfm; nlw

My Way or God's Way

Genesis 16 (read your Bible).

God tells us so much via the Word. Spoken Word, preaching; Living Word, Holy Spirit; and written Word, the Bible. We learn a lot via this means but our lives cannot change until our hearts are penetrated by this Word. We need to hear from God and He is speaking. The question is, do we want God's way or our way?

Again, we get back to will; one of our executive powers. Do we want to relinquish all our rights to God? We say we are thankful and we say we love God but our actions show conflict within our heart and mind. Even from the time our decision was made for Christ our enthusiasm has waned. We used to have a burning fire within us, now it is only embers at best.

We speak and sing of "This joy I have, the world can't take it away." It appears that is exactly what has occurred. The things of the world have clouded our vision of God.

This is also what happened with Abram if we were to continue reading Genesis 16. Abram heard God very clearly in saying he was to have a child and be the father of many nations.

The problem is its taking so long and Abram and Sarai are only getting older. Does this sound familiar? Has God promised you something but it has not materialized? A spouse, a job, peace in the valley, whatever? Have you begun to question whether or not God really promised it?

I mean, come on, you're only getting older yet things have not changed. You could say like Sarai, you are barren and it is tormenting you. So in a situation like this what do you do? You believe God, but my goodness this is taking forever. What usually occurs is your flesh comes up with a solution.

Now there is a problem with this kind of thinking. Your flesh has a solution for a spiritual problem between you and God. Since when did the flesh ever help the spiritual, especially God? Well, when you're going through something you just don't think of it this way.

So in verses 1–3, Sarai figures I will fix this problem; I know just what to do. She strongly suggests that Abram sleep with her handmaiden. Now please understand that the culture of that day was okay with this. Today's culture describes it as adultery. Culture or not it was not God's will that the promised child come via Hagar the handmaiden.

If we can just fast-forward, this fleshly idea created nothing but heartache and sorrow for everyone. Even to this day there are still repercussions from such a poor decision by Sarai and Abram.

Hagar did get pregnant. Hagar did have a child. The child was a son named Ishmael. Ishmael did get many nations but not the promised ones from God. What ultimately occurred is Sarai miraculously did have a child years later. Now the first born Ishmael and the second born Isaac had nothing but enmity for each other. To this day Ishmael's offspring (Palestinians) and Isaac's offspring (Israel) still fight and kill each other. Yes, they have the same father, but a different mother. One is the chosen people and the other is the substitute and they are not a happy camper.

Okay, let's go back now in reverse to get an understanding. God wanted to do it one way but Sarai and Abram decided to do it another way. From that poor decision the world is still reeling. Is this a perfect example of a bad choice or what? If nothing else it certainly teaches us to never pick our way over God's way. It also teaches us that the flesh never helps the spiritual.

If we don't garner this lesson, our whole life can be plagued by one poor decision after another with dire consequences. All victory and fruit will evade us due to our poor choices. Let us never think in our family or in our church; it all depends on me. Who came to that conclusion and why?

What was Sarai thinking? Think about it, God told her and Abram she would have a child. Obviously it was impossible because Sarai had long passed the flower of her youth. So now instead of leaving this impossible task in God's capable hands Sarai decides to assist him. It was all up to her so she thought.

This kind of thinking is very dangerous. It's been a long time, God is not doing it so that means I have to, really? That's what you thought? God needs my help. God has a plan, it's not happening so now I have a plan—hmm.

So God says He is going to give us a son but He is just taking too long. So we say forget it. Plan A didn't work so let's go with Plan B. So basically what you are saying is you're going to go to secondary sources for primary answers. Yep. It's obvious I can't get pregnant so let's use my young servant.

Surely you would think a wise older man like Abram would immediately shut this plan down because it's not of God. Wrong, Abram jumped on top of Hagar so fast you would have thought it was his idea all along.

How in the world can we have this mindset and expect a blessing? We go to secondary sources for primary answers. Are we now surprised by the poor results or in this case disastrous results?

Sadly even though the Bible was written centuries ago Christians today are still making poor decisions claiming they are helping God. God doesn't need or require our help.

It doesn't matter how many committee meetings, outreaches, seminars, fundraisers, or whatever we do. If God does not want it to happen it will not happen. If God wants it to happen He will send a way for it to be so. All our efforts against God's will and plan is just flapping our wings without taking flight. We can't fly; it's not God's design or way.

Now please understand we may get some results just like Sarai and Abram did. However the results won't be what we want. It can't be because it's not of God. Why do you think the church today is so weak; because it's not of God? I mean how many services can you hold and yaw still can't stop Christian divorces and broken families.

You still have Christian wayward children and teenage pregnancy right in the church. Let's get personal why don't we; You mean you're not already? Why do churches have people singing in the choir who don't go to that church or believe in God? Why does a church have a board of deacons that are known playboys? How can ten to fifteen teens get pregnant and the church remain silent like they don't see it?

I could go on but you understand where I'm going. God's ideas and plans far exceed the world. The church needs to stick with God's plans. Just because a deacon has money it doesn't make him spiritually qualified to be on the board. You get a board full of businessmen with no biblical morals and ethics. The next thing you know they put pressure on the pastor to only preach joy sermons or feel good sermons with no moral fiber.

God gives us an Isaac plan for church but we decide we are going to use an Ishmael plan. Then we wonder what went wrong. Ishmael was a fruit from the flesh decision. Isaac was the fruit from a spiritual decision. So I ask you again will it be your way or God's way?

Sarai, were you really helping God or yourself? Were you actually more concerned about Abram feelings as a man in that day without a son? You did hear God promise a son via you right, but you couldn't wait on God?

Abram, you know good and well this was not God's plan so why did you go along with it? Here was a perfect opportunity to stand up and be a man (lead) as lead by God. Well you blew that. Abram knew better but didn't do or choose better. This was basically Adam and Eve all over again.

Listening to bad counsel is one thing. Following bad counsel is something else. Church folk are hearing bad sermons. They have itching ears and want to hear certain things that make them feel good. They get rid of a good preacher or pastor because he is not giving them what they want.

It doesn't matter that the pastor is giving them what they need it's not what they want. He has to go. They will do and go along with what they know is wrong then wonder why the church can't be blessed. Families are rotten in the church and nobody can figure out why.

Unsound spiritual decisions cost us. Many times it cost our family and church too. Sometimes it cost the city, county, and the state. The Bible clearly states what is right and what is wrong. To violate it brings consequences even if you're just trying to fit the times. You can convince yourself all you want that you're doing God's will; you're helping God; you know better.

Abram made a gigantic mistake just like Adam and we are still paying for it today. This happens too often where Christians want their pastor or another person they fellowship with to say something is okay even though they know full well it's not. Just stop it.

God tells Abram he would have a son by Sarai and he would multiply his offspring from Sarai into many nations. Why would Abram think God needed help with that?

Regardless of convincing one's self that wrong is right. Faith Worth Finding Ministries with Naum Ware must at some point come to realize you simply did it your way. You did it that way because that is what you wanted to do; now own it.

Moses was told by God that He was going to free the Israelites from Egypt. God said nothing about killing a taskmaster as Moses did then hid his body in the sand. That is what Moses wanted to do because he was angry at the constant mistreatment of the taskmaster beating slaves.

So back to our story in verses 4–6, this thing really went south fast. The girl Hagar got pregnant then had a verbal altercation with Sarai. It got so heated until Sarah kicked the girl out of her tent into the hot desert.

Sarai says may the Lord judge between you and me...Really, Sarai, after you started the whole thing. You chose your way over God's way and now you boot the girl into the desert—wow? Abram you then tell Sarai, do whatever you want with Hagar; I got mines. If you want to kick her out she is your servant. Just like a man, isn't it?

So there goes Hagar to the desert. The sad, tangled web we weave by choosing our way over God's way. We cannot and we must not alter God's plans If it takes a while let it be. We must not rush it because of what we want. It's God's will, so let it be God's way.

Verses 7–16: God speaks to Hagar in trying to clean up Sarai and Abram's mess. An eighty-six-year-old man fathers a child then let's his wife kick the woman out of the tent into the desert. God tells Hagar there is water prepared for her in the desert. Although my servant Abram went about this all the wrong way and involved you in something you had nothing to do with I'm still going to bless your seed.

Now please understand something, Ms. Hagar, that boy you're going to have; oh he's going to be wild like an ass or donkey. He is going to be so full of hostility and his offspring, but I'm still going to bless you with much. (These are the Saudis, Palestinians, and so forth.) Bin Laden and company came from Ishmael and Abram is the father of all this mess. How did this happen? Because Abram did it his way?

If you check the verses God asked Hagar questions to get the answers He already knew; it was rhetorical. The answers were for her, not for God.

1. Where are you coming from?
2. Where are you going?

This made Hagar check or examine her life choices, past, present, and future.

Are you listening? This girl was utterly helpless running around in the hot dry desert. God tells her to go back to Sarai's tent and submit and He would bless her.

Paul later writes a letter to the Galatians that we should also read in Galatians 4:21–23, 28–29, please look it up in your Bible. IMPERATIVE.

When we mess up, God can fix it if we submit and obey. God can make things right that we really mess up by choosing our way over His way. God never wants to see us destroyed by our poor decisions so many times His drastic moves appear to hurt us but they are actually helping us.

Adam and Eve got kicked out of the Garden of Eden so they wouldn't have to live forever in sin by eating of the Tree of Life.

David lost his first child with Basheba even though he prayed and fasted. His son raped his own sister. Her brother then killed him. That murdering son then usurped David's throne and slept with his concubines. This is what poor decisions will do to one and his family.

I implore you, please choose God's way over your way. It makes a grave difference.

God bless you,
Fwfm; nlw

Purged with Fire

Genesis 15, NIV. (Google it.)

This is about Abram's daily trust in God. God promised him he would make him father of many nations. Abram believed this even though at the time he had no descendants. Of course Abram had some questions for God but they were about the process not unbelief. The scripture said in fact the Abram was credited righteousness due to his faith in God.

Paul repeats this in Romans 4:2, 3: "² If, in fact, Abraham was justified by works, he had something to boast about—but not before God. ³ What does Scripture say? Abraham believed God, and it was credited to him as righteousness."

Paul makes it quite clear that there is justification by grace via faith in Romans. He also makes it clear that there is deliverance from sin through the same means. Paul wants us to move away from the notion that just getting saved is sufficient; Salvation is just the beginning. He emphasizes we need to be sanctified and filled with the Holy Spirit.

This is done via a hunger for righteousness. We have to want our heart, mind, soul, and body to belong to the Lord. Many times we have to be purged by the fire of God.

So in the scripture in Genesis we have God telling Abram where he brought him from and where He is taking him to. God got his attention and made him curious due to his old age. Follow me if you will; God was actually preparing Abram for his future blessings by purging his past and present. Abram was being refined while waiting for a blessing.

God desires to do the same thing with us. As we allow the Holy Spirit to have more and more control of our lives we will be purged of all our dross. We too are already entitled because we are in Christ but sanctification or spiritual growth can be retarded (slowed) by our lack of trust and obedience.

Abram here is not commenting out of unbelief he just wanted to figure out how this was going to take place. It was like Mary when the angel told her she was going to have a child. The first thing Mary said was how can that be seeing I know not a man (I'm a virgin)? It wasn't unbelief, it was being inquisitive and in wonder.

So now in verses 9–11 it gets interesting. The first step in the process was death. A sacrifice needed to be made just like what Jesus did for us. The cross allows the Holy Spirit to enter our lives and sanctify us or make us Christ-like. Take a look at the symbolization.

The heifer represents patience and strength. The goat represents nourishment and refreshment. The ram is an image of power and vigor in battle. The birds were symbolic of gentleness and grace. Don't you find it strange that God wanted all of the animals three years old? This represents the three years Jesus spent in his public ministry. Ironically every trait above is symbolic of Jesus.

So Abram follows the directions of God and gathers the sacrifices and slays the animals. He slices everything in two but the birds and lines them up. Then something significant happens. Vultures or birds of prey swooped down and attacked the carcasses.

Abram had to aggressively drive them away. Just like the devil to try to snatch away a blessing from us; that's what these vultures represent. Satan brings with him discouragement, doubt, anger, and confusion among other negative things. We have to drive them away lest they steal or destroy our blessings.

All day, Abram is guarding the sacrificial carcasses then something else happens in verses 12–16. God is promising us that He will keep His Word but we must allow the fruit to get ripe. The time of reaping will come but we must be patient. "[11] For I know the plans I have for you," declares the Lord, "plans to prosper you and not to harm you, plans to give you hope and a future. [12] Then you will call on me and come and pray to me, and I will listen to you. God is trying to tell us some things have to happen first just trust me (Jer. 29:11, 12).

God even explains it to Abram talking about the sinful people in the land of Canaan and the Amorites. Don't you see this representing "self"? David says, "⁵ Behold, I was shapen in iniquity; and in sin did my mother conceive me" (Ps. 51:5). Basically we are reprehensible and evil apart from God. It's so foul most of us deny it; it's that horrible until we can't stand it ourselves.

We lie to ourselves and each other knowing full well we are not good people. Oh but for the blood of Christ to wash us clean. Away with the self-sufficiency and pride; Be gone jealousy, waywardness, and lust. We have some serious issues that are willful and wanton and need attention but we have been ignoring them disregarding God's Word like Eli.

We love to master others when we can't even control ourselves. We basically are a facade a hypocrite. Even our worship and praise has become routine and mechanical. Who are we praying to at alter call, the people? Are we trying to impress them or actually pray to God? Meaningless self glorifying and it shows in our living. Actions speak louder than words.

So to fix this mess, God has to purge us with fire. God has Abram to offer this sacrifice and look at what happened in verses 17–21. A miracle of deliverance shows up out of mass confusion and despair. You see once Abram realized he was helpless and under constant attack by the devil God stepped in.

We too must realize we are enslaved by sin and selfishness. For the most part we have been deceived by ourselves, our ego and our pride. Our church tells us we have the answer yet it doesn't show in our lives. We're just as bad as the world in divorce, living, and everything else yet we claim to have the answer.

Victory only comes when we surrender our cold empty hearts and allow them to be filled with the love of God via Christ and the Holy Spirit. Sometimes for this to happen we have to reach our breaking point; we have to have a crisis. This makes way for God to purge us and prepare us.

God moved in formed as a smoking firepot with a blazing torch and passed through the sacrificial animals pieces. His presence refined or purged the pieces just like He wants to do to our hearts. God broke through Abram's darkness and shined his great light into Abram's life.

This pattern is not unusual; the same thing happened to Jacob before he met his brother Esau at the brook Peniel. The angel of the Lord wrestles with him and broke his hip.

"It was then that the blazing lamp of God shined into Jacob's dark heart and purged him or refined him" (Gen. 32:24–32).

How about David when Nathan came to him after he committed adultery with Bathsheba and killed her husband. David confessed his sin to God and the piercing light of God shined into his dark heart.

Paul is another example out killing Christians thinking he is doing the right thing or the will of God. God encounters him on the road to Damascus and blinds him for three days (Acts 9:1–19). Again, the bright lamp of God broke into a dark heart to purge and refine it. This proud Pharisee finally saw the light.

Can you now see yourself in any of these examples? Maybe it is latent sin in our life and now it is exposed? Maybe it is divorce or job loss but suddenly you realize God is shining a bright light into your life. You can no longer skirt him via justification, rationalization, or excuses. No more Popeye excuses of "I am what I am."

You are what you are and now you can see it clearly as God's smoking firepot and blazing torch has burned up the dross. The furnace of God has heated up and brought a light into your life so nothing is hidden. There is a reason for this; figure it out. I ask you now do you have a moral cancer eating away at you? Do you have too much pride like Lucifer? Are you holding a grudge against someone and refuse to forgive them?

The lamp of God is shining bright on you passing through whatever it is to purge it and refine you. It's high time you come face to face with God's light. God is going to make sure every hidden corner of your life is exposed to uncover your darkness and purge you like Adam in the garden.

What God wants is to not be a caldron to you but instead a guiding lamp so you can see your way; it's your choice. God wants His truth to penetrate our dark hearts and turn us away from anything amiss. Just because something is shiny or pretty doesn't make it good; the fire will show what it really is. Through the flames of God He will purge or dissipate all our fears and increase our faith.

God is trying to tell us to stop denying, defending and protecting what we want and accept what we need. Wrong is wrong it can't be justified. If we keep playing with it we become defiled and polluted all in our soul.

Have you wondered why there is so much confusion in some lives and so many churches, the vultures are circling? Bitterness, strife, vain glory, envy, self-righteousness, and so on. These happen because we refuse to purge them by instead inviting the fruits of the Spirit in Galatians 5. We cater to evil and it then envelops us. We give old wrong room and board in our heart and mind then we can't evict it.

It ruins and wrecks our place and we have no recourse because we gave it permission to be there. God had to come in with a fiery furnace and burn it out (drive) of our life.

So now that we have discovered whatever enemies within have you also discovered God via Christ is greater? "4 Ye are of God, little children, and have overcome them: because greater is he that is in you, than he that is in the world" (1 John 4:4).

God does what we could not or would not or refused to do to our enemies. He attacks and destroys all our inner temptations which oppose our spiritual growth. Through the smoking firepot of God and the burning torch God purges us and sets us free. This is so far past just salvation.

Too many of us think just to be saved is enough; we think just to know Christ is sufficient. We couldn't be further from the truth. We have to be sanctified (cleaned up by the Spirit) to truly experience the peace and joy of the Lord.

So now I ask you, would you rather the furnace or the lamp of God? Once you give your life to Him one of them is coming. Will it be the furnace or the lamp? (Look at Psalm 119:105.) If you think you can serve two masters and still dabble with the world you're going to get burned by the fiery furnace of God.

God will burn up your relationships, money, job, habits, you name it. Whatever is keeping you from spiritual growth God will send His fiery furnace.

God wants us to see ourselves for what we really are and this can only happen via being purged by the fire. It's a hard thing watching a man or woman admit their shortcomings.

If you want the promised land of God, to take possession you must be prepared via being purged, burned in the fiery caldron of God, or set free. This will purify us or prepare us to receive God's blessings.

The Word says you cannot put new wine in old skins... God will reveal to us the true nature of our heart and deliver us from ourselves. Too many of us are holding ourselves as prisoners and we haven't even realized it. We are keeping ourselves from whatever promises God has in store for us because we're too caught up in self. May the purging begin so we can be set free.

God bless you,
Fwfm; nlw

Tell Your Heart to Beat Again

There was a pastor who had a heart surgeon who went to his church. One of the things this pastor wanted to do was to see a heart surgery take place. When the day of the surgery came, they rolled the patient in. They began to cut her chest cavity open took her heart out and began to repair it.

One of the things they do is they have to restart the heart again before they close the chest. As they began to do the procedures to start the heart, the heart wouldn't start. The doctor then did something so out of textbook that is not written down, something that you really don't do.

He got down on his knees and he said, "Ms. Johnson, this is your doctor. We have fixed your heart. There is nothing wrong with your heart. Ms. Johnson, if you can hear me I need you to tell your heart to beat again; and her heart began to beat."

Why do I share this story with you, because the great physician has fixed your heart and my heart, yet I find it interesting that sometimes we allow the voice of the enemy to whisper to us louder than the voice of our father. It seems like some of these voices tell us you're in a situation you'll never recover from. Or what you did you will never be forgiven.

Perhaps somebody did something to you and you can't forgive them. But I'm here to tell you that you can forgive. You can and you will get back up again. You will get another job. God will fix you then either that relationship or with someone else will be with you. You can and will move forward with your life; you don't have to walk with a limp.

It's like what this doctor told this lady. You have to come into agreement. The heart was already repaired. God has fixed your problem now you have to come into agreement and accept God's grace and mercy. You have to tell you heart to beat again.

I look at my situation of having lost my first granddaughter recently oh did it sting; it hurt. I said how could God do this to my family; to my son and his wife? I fully realize God doesn't have to answer our questions but he gives us room to vent. I needed to vent because of this precious child. I couldn't function; I felt numb, I didn't even want to go on. God spoke to me and said, leave this to me. Enjoy Ryanne's twin brother Lincoln and tell your heart to beat again.

I'm the great physician; I'm your Father. I need you to believe and trust. I know the pain you feel in loss of a loved one, but I need you to trust me and go on; tell your heart to beat again.

> You're shattered, like you've never been before
> The life you knew, in a thousand pieces on the floor
> And words fall short in times like these, when this world drives you to your knees
> You think you're never gonna get back, to the you that used to be
>
> [Chorus]
> Tell your heart to beat again
> Close your eyes and breathe it in
> Let the shadows fall away
> Step into the light of grace
> Yesterday's a closing door
> You don't live there anymore
> Say goodbye to where you've been
> And tell your heart to beat again
>
> Beginning, just let that word wash over you
> It's alright now, love's healing hands have pulled you through

So get back up, take step one, leave the darkness,
feel the sun
'Cause your story's far from over and your journey's just begun

[Chorus]
Tell your heart to beat again
Close your eyes and breathe it in
Let the shadows fall away
Step into the light of grace
Yesterday's a closing door
You don't live there anymore
Say goodbye to where you've been
And tell your heart to beat again

[Bridge]
Let every heartbreak and every scar
Be a picture that reminds you who has carried
you this far
'Cause love sees farther than you ever could
In this moment heaven's working, everything for
your good

Please tell your heart to beat again.
Half of this message is from Danny Gokey, Tell
Your Heart To Beat Again.
Thanks, Danny.

God bless you,
Fwfm; nlw

A Mother's Prayer

"And she was in bitterness of soul, and prayed unto the Lord, and wept sore. And she vowed a vow, and said, O Lord of hosts, if thou wilt indeed look on the affliction of thine handmaid, and remember me, and not forget thine handmaid, but wilt give unto thine handmaid a man-child, then I will give him unto the Lord all the days of his life."
—1 Samuel 1:10–11

Hannah, the mother of Samuel, is a great example of a praying mother. Her child's birth was an answer to prayer; his dedication to the work of the Lord was the result of a covenant made with God in prayer: and no doubt Samuel's remarkable life was the answer to the unceasing prayers of his godly mother.

I could give you a list of the great men whose mothers have been prayer warriors, because the history of great and good men is simply a list of praying mothers, and there is hardly an exception to this rule. If mothers don't pray today, God help their children for our times are hard.

The highest example of moral conviction in a man of American heritage was in our most noted president, "Honest Abe." Abraham Lincoln's (1809–1865) mother was a godly Christian who, every Sunday, set Abe on her knee and read to him the Word of God. As most mothers of that time, her emphasis for her son was the knowledge of the Ten Commandments.

This godly mother once said, "I would rather Abe be able to read the Bible than to own a farm, if he can have only one." Nancy Lincoln died in 1818, when Abe was only nine years of age, but the law of God had been inscribed in his heart. Her last words were: Abe,

I'm going to leave you now, and I shall not return. I want you to be kind to your father and live as I have taught you. Love your Heavenly Father and keep His commandments.

When asked later in life why he was so honest, he said that he could still clearly hear the tones of his mother's voice as she spoke to him from Exodus 20 and read of the Lord God who gave His commandments. Lincoln declared, "All that I am or hope to be, I owe to my angel mother." This information is printed in so many books and we need to use it for our benefit today.

So not only can women bring children into the world but they can also sustain their lives by giving them a relationship with their heavenly father. This is why home Bible study is so important. This is why Sunday school is so important. This is why BTU or Bible Training Union is so important.

Whether mom taught us to say a scripture before each meal or recite a scripture before going to bed, mom was on the right track. You see, mothers prepare us for the long haul, not just the right now. The fervent desire of a mother's perseverance in teaching her children is almost godlike; she really cares for the welfare of her children. This is what Hannah did in preparing Samuel for the Lord.

In this so-called modern day of church the emphasis is not put on family or mothering as in the past and look at the results. We need mother's prayers and input We need a relationship with God. When prayer was in school there were no school shootings. When mom disciplined children, there were no school shootings. We need moms to pray.

If our lives are going to be changed, it is going to start with the prayer of our mothers. As the old song writer said, Mother was there when I went to school; it was mother who taught the Golden Rule…

If we intend to prevail or succeed in life it will start with a praying mother. We cannot afford to act like mom's prayers don't matter because even the slightest ones probably saved us from troubles unknown.

Let's take this opportunity to start our relationship with God via our Christian mother. As the Word says, the fear of the Lord (respect or reverence) is the beginning of wisdom. The influence of

Motherhood is not only an opportunity; it is also a responsibility. It prepares us for not only this world but our own family to raise later in life. How terrible to have a nonpraying mother. The church today and the world show us so many examples of this. Bless God for a mother's prayer for without her where would we be?

May we be pricked in our hearts to not only hear our mother's prayer but allow God to answer it with our changed lives? May we then grow up to be an asset to society and not a deficit in Jesus name, amen.

God bless you,
HAPPY MOTHER'S DAY
Fwfm; nlw

Anchored in the Lord

If a boat is not anchored, it is tossed by the wind and waves of the sea or ocean. Every captain of the boat knows his anchor must always be in tact when he goes out to deep waters. It is the same thing when it comes to spiritual matters. We are the captain of our souls. Life gets deep even when we thought it was going to stay shallow. The question is what is the shape of our anchor? Do we even have an anchor?

One thing we cannot do is obtain an anchor in the storm. We have to already have an anchor. You don't look for an umbrella in the rain; you have it with you in preparation and simply put it up when needed. The songwriter said in times like these, we need an anchor.

> In times like these you need a Savior,
> In times like these you need an anchor;
> Be very sure, be very sure,
> Your anchor holds and grips the Solid Rock!
>
> This Rock is Jesus, Yes He's the One,
> This Rock is Jesus, the only One;
> Be very sure, be very sure,
> Your anchor holds and grips the Solid Rock!
>
> In times like these you need the Bible,
> In times like these, O be not idle;
> Be very sure, be very sure,
> Your anchor holds and grips the Solid Rock!
>
> This Rock is Jesus, Yes He's the One,
> This Rock is Jesus, the only One;

Be very sure, be very sure,
Your anchor holds and grips the Solid Rock!

Without Jesus, we are weak and pitiful. Not only will we struggle and gasp through life; we more than likely will drown. Our faith is attacked as we experience each storm and we find out just how good our anchor is. Troubles have a tendency to increase, but the question is how about our faith in God? Does it get weaker with every storm and every trial as it drags us through all sorts of anguish?

Do we lose hope in God and start to look for more accessible or reasonable ways to resolve our troubles? How strong is our anchor? Do we really believe God has some divine purpose in our trials as James says or do we instead believe God has forgotten about us?

Should we shift our thoughts to the Lord in our storm or should we in panic grab whatever anchor we can as long as it looks steady? Think about it, how wise is it to grab a hold of a faulty anchor in times of a storm. To give in to our doubts and then reach out to a bad anchor is to have a spiritually uncertain life that will no doubt be tossed and driven by the storms of life. How much wiser and better it would be to anchor ourselves in the Lord and His Word. We can then ride out whatever our storm is in the peace of God. Listen you will lose jobs. You will get divorced or your parents will. You are your loved ones will get sick. You will lose loved ones and you will be bereaved? Depending on your preparation these can be storms of life. Are you prepared, do you have an anchor?

Let me give you the lyrics of this last song I used to sing in church all the time. It will help you in your time of storm. Please Google it so you can hear it for yourself and be blessed and encouraged. My soul has been anchored in the storm (Douglas Miller).

Though the storms keep on raging in my life
And sometimes it's hard to tell the night from day
Still that hope that lies within is reassured as I keep my eyes upon the distant shore
I know He'll lead me safely to that blessed place
He has prepared

But if the storm don't cease and if the winds keep
on blowing in my life
My soul has been anchored in the Lord.

VERSE:
I realize that sometimes, in this life, we're gonna
be tossed by the waves and the
currents that seem so fierce
But in the Word of God—I've got an anchor, oh
yes I have, and keeps me steadfast,
unmovable, despite the tide
But if the storm don't cease and if the winds keep
on blowing in my life
My soul has been anchored in the Lord.

God bless you,
Fwfm; nlw

I'm Going Through

It can be very hard to be thankful or grateful when all around us is constant turmoil. People keep saying be thankful—seriously? How can we be thankful for one trying circumstance after another? We have asked God to remove a situation and yet it still exists. Now you want me to give thanks?

This is where the Word comes in so handy. The Bible helps us see what we could not see on your own. It also helps us discover value in our adversities. Yes, with God to help we can show appreciation even during our trials. Let's look at a few things to help us be able to say "I'm going through."

1. We have to really believe God. We have to really trust God because our faith will be tried. Our biblical perspective and perception has to be on point. Many times God has purpose in our trials. This is very hard for us to bear. Without being led by the Holy Spirit we can miss this and become bitter. Instead of using our limited wisdom we need to rely on God's wisdom. We can ask or question the "why" all day long but it doesn't help us.

2. Either we believe God is working for our good and his purpose or not Perhaps if we look at it this way as coming from a loving God either sent or allowed it can help us. "28 And we know that all things work together for good to them that love God, to them who are the called according to his purpose" (Rom. 8:28). (However, please do not tell someone who just lost a loved one this; it's inappropriate though applicable).

"The Lord is my light and my salvation; whom shall I fear? The Lord is the strength of my life; of whom shall I be afraid?" (Ps. 27:1).

"[14] Wait on the Lord: be of good courage, and he shall strengthen thine heart: wait, I say, on the Lord" (Ps. 27:14).

Therefore humble yourselves under the mighty hand of God, that He may exalt you in due time, casting all your care upon Him, for He cares for you (Pet. 5:6, 7).

"Cast your burden on the Lord, and He shall sustain you; He shall never permit the righteous to be moved" (Ps. 55:22).

"The righteous cry out, and the Lord hears, and delivers them out of all their troubles" (Ps. 34:17).

3. No one said we had to like our circumstances but we do need to submit them to God. Trying to carry the burden ourselves is just not prudent. Just because God allows or permits trials in our life doesn't take away from his goodness. Remember he also said, "[2] When thou passest through the waters, I will be with thee; and through the rivers, they shall not overflow thee: when thou walkest through the fire, thou shalt not be burned; neither shall the flame kindle upon thee" (Isa. 43:2).

What's going to help us get through our issues is having confidence in God's love and guidance, also his care. All of this helps us be able to say; I'm going through instead of giving up.

Lastly, rely on God's strength and not your own. If anyone can help us endure it would be God. Don't be so quick to drop God and pick up foolishness like that is a panacea. Be grateful for the love of God. Show appreciation by relying on him and not using sin as a crutch. "[5] Trust in the Lord with all thine heart; and lean not unto thine own understanding. [6] In all thy ways acknowledge him, and he shall direct thy paths" (Prov. 3:5).

Allow God to alter your frame of mind. Pray about it and realize God can change you or the situation. Always leave the outcome to God; do not run off ahead of him.

God bless you,
Fwfm; nlw

True Praise and Worship

When you really love someone it prompts you to action. I know this because God so loved the world that he gave his only begotten Son. Did you see that? God, a noun (person, place, or thing), gave (a verb or action word) his only Son (a gift of love). Love prompts action.

If you truly delight in the Lord you ought to show it by how you live, not just how you talk. Take a look at Psalm 37:3–5:

> ³ Trust in the Lord, and do good; so shalt thou dwell in the land, and verily thou shalt be fed.
> ⁴ Delight thysetf also in the Lord: and he shall give thee the desires of thine heart.
> ⁵ Commit thy way unto the Lord; trust also in him; and he shall bring it to pass.

Instead of trying to get "stuff" from the Lord as instructed by the "Joy Boys" or televangelist so you can send them money try going by the Word instead. Trust God, delight yourself in God or seek God, then commit yourself to Him. Show God that you want a relationship with him more than anything.

True praise is an active faith. It's greater than emotion. True praise challenges us to leave old paths and the things the "old man" did. Our heart is regenerated: we become a new creature. We understand as John said our problem is the world, the flesh and the devil. Who will we yield to God or the prior. We must stop claiming to praise God yet we yield to the crooked.

Our real struggle is always with our executive power of the will or self. Will we flow with the current or fight it to really praise God? The more we try to follow the Word and trust God and delight ourselves in Him and commit ourselves to Him, here comes the distractions of the world.

Many times it happens right in the alleged house of God, the church. Short dresses, tight dresses, low cut blouses, loose hips and large hips God is calling us out of complacency to commitment, a higher way of thinking. The question is will we answer the call or ignore God yet still claim to praise him?

Just remember this God will never leave us where he found us or where we are. This is the reason He wants us to delight in Him; it changes us, we become more like Him. This is why the scripture beckons us in Proverb 3:5, 6.

> [5] Trust in the Lord with all your heart,
> And lean not on your own understanding;
> [6] In all your ways acknowledge Him,
> And He shall direct your paths.

It's not for Him it's for us. Do you want what your heart wants or do you want Jesus more than anything? May your heart be regenerated to want and praise what is proper that would be Jesus.

Look at what the Word says in Psalms 104:1–10, 13–15, 19–20, and 24. We worship and praise God because He made everything; it only makes sense. We praise Him for his greatness He alone is King (read Psalms 145:1–7).

Nothing is too hard for our God why won't we praise him. Look at what he did to Egypt for his loved one Israel. How could we not praise him; who is like our God? He reigns. Our God is an awesome God; He reigns from Heaven above.

God bless you,
Fwfm; nlw

More Than Anything

^{11–13} It happened that as he made his way toward Jerusalem, he crossed over the border between Samaria and Galilee. As he entered a village, ten men, all lepers, met him. They kept their distance but raised their voices, calling out, "Jesus, Master, have mercy on us!"

^{14–16} Taking a good look at them, he said,
"Go, show yourselves to the priests."

—Luke 17:11–19, The Message

They went, and while still on their way, became clean. One of them, when he realized that he was healed, turned around, and came back, shouting his gratitude, glorifying God. He kneeled at Jesus's feet, so grateful. He couldn't thank him enough—and he was a Samaritan.

> ^{17–19} Jesus said, "Were not ten healed? Where are the nine? Can none be found to come back and give glory to God except this outsider?" Then he said to him, "Get up. On your way. Your faith has healed and saved you."

Can I just preach to you for a few minutes? This is such a great story and so full of blessings for us. Please understand lepers had to be separated from society so no one else would be contaminated. A group of them saw Jesus coming and cried out to him for help as he passed by. Jesus heard their cries and healed them and one of them came back to him in gratitude.

Now let's decipher this. Ten men were healed but only one returned to say thank you. So nine men could ask for help but then when they get it never show gratitude; remind you of anyone? You know God does not like ingrates. To show how appreciative Jesus was of the ones who came back; not only did he get healed he also got saved.

You know what this reminds me of? A song by Natalie Grant. She had cancer and cried to Jesus and he healed her. Her cancer went into remission. Natalie then wrote a song called "More Than Anything." The lyrics are attached here.

> I know if You wanted to You could wave Your hand
> Spare me this heartache, and change Your plan
> And I know any second You could take my pain away
> But even if You don't, I pray
>
> [Chorus]
> Help me want the Healer More than the healing
> Help me want the Saviour More than the saving
> Help me want the Giver More than the giving
> Oh help me want You Jesus More than anything
>
> [Verse 2]
> You know more than anyone that my flesh is weak
> And You know I'd give anything for a remedy
> And I'll ask a thousand more times to set me free today
> Oh but even if You don't, I pray
>
> [Chorus]
> Help me want the Healer More than the healing
> Help me want the Saviour More than the saving
> Help me want the Giver More than the giving
> Oh help me want You Jesus More than anything

Do you see the parallel here, this leper wanted more than the healing, he wanted Jesus and he got him. In life we become so distracted by what we are given we forget who gave it people don't want

God until they are dying; they have no use for Jesus. They are content with the jobs, homes, cars, clothes, and etc.

We must make better choices in life to our whole future not just the present distractions have hurt too many people; must we be in that crowd. Let's change that even now and be thankful, be grateful and seek Jesus. He wants a relationship with us to help us. Will we deny him at our peril? I don't know about you but I want Jesus more than anything.

Please Google the song "More Than Anything" (by Natalie Grant) and go ahead and let it bring you to tears.

God bless you,
Fwfm; nlw

Confidence in God

When you sit on a chair you certainly trust that it will hold you. When you take a vehicle on a far journey you trust that it will get you there and back. What about when you trust a friend, a loved one with your confidential information believing they are going to help you? How did that work out?

The beautiful thing with God is we can trust him at all times in all things. Life has a way of draining us mentally, physically, emotionally, and spiritually. God knows that and has said over and over again, lean weary one upon my breast. Come unto me all ye that labour and are heavy laden and I will give you rest.

Song writers have said, "Take your burdens to the Lord and leave it here." God is more than willing to support us and give us strength if we but release our problems to him. Jesus said give it to me I'll bear it; give it to me I'll share it. If there is a need in your life just give it to me.

Instead of trying to do everything in our own effort or strength we can find rest in God. We must have the confidence in God that He will in fact sustain us. Read Psalms 55 in The Voice version.

Hear me, O God.
Tune Your ear to my plea,
and do not turn Your face from my prayer.
² Give me Your attention.
Answer these sighs of sorrow;
my troubles have made me restless—I groan from anxiety
³ All because of my enemy! Because his voice speaks against me,

his wickedness torments me!
He casts down misfortune upon me;
his anger flares; his grudges grow against me.
4 My heart seizes within my chest; I am in anguish!
I am terrified my life could end on any breath.
5 I shiver and shudder in fear;
I can't stop because this horror is just too much.
6 I said, "If only my arms were wings like the dove's!
I would fly away from here and find rest—
7 Yes, I would venture far
and weave a nest in the wilderness.
8 "I would rush to take refuge
away from the violent storm and pounding winds."
9 Throw them off, O Lord. Confuse their speech, and frustrate their plans,
for violence and contention are building within the city.
I can see it with my own eyes.
10 They plot day and night, scurrying the city walls like rats, trouble and evil lurking everywhere.
11 In the heart of the city, destruction awaits.
Oppression and lies swarm the streets,
and they will not take leave; no, they will not go.
12 If it were just an enemy sneering at me,
I could take it.
If it were just someone who has always hated me, treating me like dirt, I'd simply hide away.
13 But it is you! A man like me, my old friend, my companion.
14 We enjoyed sweet conversation, walking together in the house of God among the pressing crowds.
15 Let death sneak up on them, swallow them alive into the pit of death.

Why? Because evil stirs in their homes; evil is all around them.

[16] But I, I shall call upon God,

and by His word, the Eternal shall save me.

[17] Evening, morning, and noon I will plead;

I will grumble and moan before Him until He hears my voice.

[18] And He will rescue my soul, untouched, plucked safely from the battle,

despite the many who are warring against me.

[19] God, enthroned from ancient times through eternity, will hear my prayers and strike them down.

For they have refused change; they supply their every need and have no fear of God.

[20] My friend has become a foe, breaking faith, tearing down peace. He's betrayed our covenant.

[21] Oh, how his pleasant voice is smoother than butter, while his heart is enchanted by war.

Oh, how his words are smoother than oil, and yet each is a sword drawn in his hand.

[22] Cast your troubles/burden upon the Lord;

His care will sustain you.

He will not allow His righteous to be shaken.

[23] But You, O God, You will drive them into the lowest pit. Violent, lying people won't live beyond their middle years. (Ps. 55:1–23)

But I place my trust in You.

God ahead and Google the song "Take Your Burdens to the Lord."

God bless you,
Fwfm; nlw

Did Not Our Lord Tell the Disciples…?

> [45] Then He opens their minds so they can comprehend the meaning of the Hebrew Scriptures.
>
> Jesus: [46] This is what the Scriptures said: that the promised Anointed One should suffer and rise from the dead on the third day, [47] that in His name a radical change of thought and life should be preached, and that in His name the forgiveness of sins should be preached, beginning in Jerusalem and extending to all nations. [48] You have witnessed the fulfillment of these things. [49] So I am sending My Father's promise to you. Stay in the city until you receive it—until power from heaven comes upon you.
>
> —Luke 24:45–49

It's Resurrection Sunday and God is trying to tell us something. The church is full. People have come today who have not been to church since Christmas. This may be our only opportunity to reach them. God is trying to tell us something—listen.

The more we give room to the Word through faith; the Holy Spirit can lead, guide and teach us. We must have the power of the Spirit to reach ourselves and others. We are to remain where we are until we receive power from on high. Where are you going to get this power?

Are you watching TV, movies, Internet? What are you watching? Are you reading the Word, fasting and praying; is your heart burning from the power of the Spirit? Are you sharing with others what God has done for you and through you?

Did you notice the gifts that the apostle Paul says Jesus sent after He ascended apostles, prophets, evangelists, pastors, and teachers?

> "[9] Notice that it says he returned to heaven. This means that he had first come down from the heights of heaven, far down to the lowest parts of the earth. [10] The same one who came down is the one who went back up, that he might fill all things everywhere with himself, from the very lowest to the very highest.
>
> "[11] Some of us have been given special ability as apostles; to others he has given the gift of being able to preach well; some have special ability in winning people to Christ, helping them to trust him as their Savior; still others have a gift for caring for God's people as a shepherd does his sheep, leading and teaching them in the ways of God.
>
> "[12] Why is it that he gives us these special abilities to do certain things best? It is that God's people will be equipped to do better work for him, building up the Church, the body of Christ, to a position of strength and maturity." (Eph. 4:9–12)

The more we listen to the counsel of the Holy Spirit and the Word of God the more our faith is built up and we become more intimate with Christ. This is necessary if we are going to survive in the world. Keep in mind it is our faith that Satan is after to rob from us. When we go through "stuff" Satan doesn't want our jobs, our money, our mates, or our children. Satan is after our faith.

We live by our faith; that is what the Word says. "[4] Behold, his soul which is lifted up is not upright in him: but the just shall live by his faith" (Hab. 2:4). "[38]Now the just shall live by faith: but if any man drawback, my soul shall have no pleasure in him" (Heb. 10:38).

> "[4] For whatsoever is born of God overcometh the world: and this is the victory that overcometh the

world, even our faith" (1 John 5:4). What is the
victory that overcomes the world; our faith, that
bears repeating. So don't get it twisted, victory in
this world is not just love like so many have said.
Love is defined in so many different ways.

According to the Word the answer is Christian faith. We believe
that God is ultimately in charge and will make the final decision in
everything because He so loved us that He gave his only begotten
Son to us. We accept this by faith.

You see, Satan could care less about what we have; he simply
wants to attack our faith. If he can't steal our soul at least he can
destroy our faith. Will you let him? We have to stop going to church
for the choir or how the preacher moves so charismatically. The
major question is can the church we attend build up the saints and
make us stronger in Christ?

In order for us to believe the Word and be effective just like
Christ used the Holy Spirit, we too will need the Spirit. Our whole
relationship with God is based upon faith and the aid of the Holy
Spirit.

We do not give faith and the Holy Spirit the credit they deserve.
The Spirit builds our faith by leading us, guiding us teaching us, protecting us and so forth. The Holy Spirit even prays with and for us,
telling us what to say based on our need.

God only deals with us based on our faith and the Holy Spirit
preps us for that. We must thank God for his Spirit.

The whole reason the Holy Spirit is here is to assist us or build
up the body of Christ. The power of Christ is attributed into the lives
of men and women through their faith. One preacher said a saint's
life is in the hands of God as a bow and arrow is in the hands of an
archer.

With our faith giving God power over us God is stretching and
aiming at something even we cannot see or understand. Even when
we think we cannot stand anymore God continues to stretch us until
He lets it fly and whoosh-hits His mark. We must keep in mind we
are here as a part of God's design not our own. "[28]And we know that

all things work together for good to them that love God, to them who are the called according to his purpose" (Rom. 8:28).

This is the problem in the church today. We forget it's not about us, it's about HIM. It's not about us. it's for us. The whole purpose of the church is to build us up spiritually. It is not about committees, choirs, meetings, and positions in the church. Who cares where you sit?

What kind of decisions are you making for yourself and your family? Have you fully surrendered yourself to Christ; your faith will tell off on you.

God bless you,
Fwfm; nlw

Behold Your God

Who has scooped up the ocean in his two hands,
or measured the sky between his thumb and little
finger,
Who has put all the earth's dirt in one of his
baskets,
weighed each mountain and hill?
Who could ever have told GOD what to do or
taught him his business?
What expert would he have gone to for advice,
what school would he attend to team justice?
What god do you suppose might have taught
him what he knows,
showed him how things work?

—Isaiah 40:12–14

Have you not known?
Have you not heard?
The everlasting God, the Lord,
The Creator of the ends of the earth,
Neither faints nor is weary.
His understanding is unsearchable.
29 He gives power to the weak,
And to those who have no might He increases
strength.
30 Even the youths shall faint and be weary,
And the young men shall utterly fall,

³¹ But those who wait on the Lord Shall renew
their strength;
They shall mount up with wings like eagles,
They shall run and not be weary,
They shall walk and not faint.

—Verses 28–31

Listen; When you pass through the waters, I will
be with you;
And through the rivers, they shall not overflow
you.
When you walk through the fire, you shall not
be burned,
Nor shall the flame scorch you.

—Isaiah 43:2

"Do not remember the former things,
Nor consider the things of old.
Behold, I will do a new thing,
Now it shall spring forth;
Shall you not know it?
I will even make a road in the wilderness
And rivers in the desert.

—Isaiah 43:18, 19

Now listen, readers, I need you to Google this song and listen to it entirely and behold your God. "So You Would Know" by the Brooklyn Tabernacle Choir.

God bless you,
Fwfm; nlw

Behold His Glory

What a journey from Egypt to Canaan. All the way through the wilderness with only those under twenty years old making it to the Promised Land. The chains of Egypt were strong but what was in the hearts of the people was even stronger. Moses had to remind the people of who they were and whose they were.

Moses also reminded the people that they owed allegiance and obedience to God. Were they going to be faithful and committed to the glory of God or not? This is what God had Moses to write in Deuteronomy 29:29: "29 The secret things belong unto the Lord our God: but those things which are revealed belong unto us and to our children forever; that we may do all the words of this law." Are there unanswered questions? Yes. Some things are not for us to know; the answer belongs to God. What we do know is we need to respect who God is and give him glory.

How many times and in how many ways must God reveal himself? He gave so many people a better life showing his majesty and holiness. Did it cause them to behold his glory, no?

How long can we ignore who God is and yet claim to know him? The problem is not in recognition of who God is; the issue is giving him his due respect. Even today we give more respect to judges, politicians, movie stars, and sports people than God. What have these people done for us?

Something has our attention or someone. It would behoove us to behold God for who he is while he is our Lord and Savior and not our judge. We are dealing with power and depth like none in the world. I beseech you brethren by the mercies of God; behold his glory.

Answer me this, do we ignore God because to acknowledge him would mean we are obligated to obedience? So you mean to tell me it is better to remain in ignorance denying the power and depth of God simply because his Word pierces and judges us?

Did you know that the mysteries of God are far more satisfying than the so-called solution of man? Like Psalm 131 we would do good to drop our pride and behold God's glory like a child. Remember being a child in the big old world; how fascinating it was and how small we were?

> "Lord, my heart is not haughty, nor mine eyes lofty: neither do I exercise myself in great matters, or in things too high for me.
> "2 Surely I have behaved and quieted myself, as a child that is weaned of his mother my soul is even as a weaned child.
> "3 Let Israel hope in the Lord from henceforth and forever."

Have we now become too big, too smart, and too busy to behold the glory of God? We would be making the same mistake as Satan; thinking too much of who we are and what we have accomplished. Also at the same time thinking too little of God.

Paul tells us in Romans 11:33–34 just how insignificant we are compared to God.

> "33 O the depth of the riches both of the wisdom and knowledge of God! How unsearchable are his judgments, and his ways past finding out!
> "34 For who hath known the mind of the Lord? Or who hath been his counselor?"

Don't let Bible study fool you; God's Word and God himself are wonders we behold and marvel not just subjects we master.

It's not about trying to be theologically smart or know all the answers; it's really about knowing God himself and giving him glory.

God bless you,
Fwfm; nlw

Who Am I, Really?

Many times God is trying to tell us something. Why can't we hear Him? Perhaps it's because our hearing is impaired in the sounds of the world. There is so much happening around us until it's hard to hear God unless we are finely tuned into His Word and Spirit.

Isn't it funny how we can talk about keeping our enemies, the world, the flesh and the devil away from us? We talk about not being deceived. We never thought for a second we could be deceiving ourselves. Just think about it, just because you say something and say you mean it; do you really?

It's so easy to say we must not justify, rationalize, or excuse our behavior but the real question is, have we? That is where the deception takes place. In trying to protect ourselves we allow certain things figuring, well I'm at least owed this… Who are we really?

God wants to give us discernment according to His Word but the question is, are we ready to receive it or are we blocking our own blessings? John the Baptist went around preaching the unadulterated gospel. It was so raw the Kings wife ordered his head. John the Baptist was trying to get people to understand the power of God via his Son Jesus Christ.

The crowd, and that was including the religious leaders, were not ready for that message. They did not want retrospection; no we don't need to look inside ourselves, we are pure. Are you really? You say that but what does your life show? Are you deceiving yourselves because you certainly are not deceiving God?

John told some of the folks when they went to church it wasn't so much to praise God or worship God but to find out what he was doing and why the crowd was following him. John then went on to say they needed to repent because they were a network of snakes (Matt. 3:1–12).

Yeah, not quite what they wanted to hear; who among you is ready for the truth? The Word says you shall know the truth and it will set you free. What if you thought you were already free now this preacher is telling you that you're in sinful bondage by choice? Off with that's preacher's head. Okay, and who are you really?

Please tell me what is going on with the doctrine of the church now. We look just like the schools. Remember when the school used to have prayer and no shootings? Yeah the politicians we put in decided we didn't need prayer or corporal punishment and just look how that worked out. Cultivate and saturate your heart and mind with His Word. That Word is so strong, so double edged like a sword until it will cut going and coming. No man can meet Christ and stay the same.

I ask you what can be more important or more valuable in this life than a close relationship with God. Our lives are filled with circumstances that try our faith daily and call for spiritual discernment Some of this stuff we are not going to get out of immediately; it's going to take patience and wisdom.

God is calling on us to spend some quality time with Him via prayer, His Word, and the Holy Spirit. He wants to open our eyes and our heart to be receptive to discernment. The question is will we put down the worlds toys and give God a chance. Not only so will we be patient in waiting for God's answers.

The world has microwaved us to think everything can come right now, NO, sometimes we have to wait on the Lord. Can you say, I don't mind waiting on the Lord? I challenge you today to look at the man or woman in the mirror and answer the question; who am I, really?

Then ask God to order your steps and show you where to walk. Tell God, "Lord, remove the enemy presence from my life even if the enemy is me. Hide me in your love, grace and mercy. Oh Bless, God."

Fwfm; nlw

Why Do We Pray?

It has been often asked, does God really hear our prayers? I have been going through this for such a long time and I have prayed so many prayers and still here I am. Yes, God does hear and answer prayer. These are His answers—yes, no, not right now. The problem is many times we do not like the answer we receive.

We pray because God told us to. He said talk to me and learn of me. Learn what I need from you so you can hear me and find help in your time of need. How can we hear if we do not know His Word? It's ironic how we spend hours watching TV, on the computer, or at the movies. Oh, but when it comes time to pray that should only take a few minutes, God knows my heart.

Can we just get an understanding of who we are talking to for clarification? Old Testament referred to God as YAHWEH—a term meaning I AM or One who never changes. God was also referred to as ELOHIM, speaking of God's sovereignty. When this term was used they were speaking of their confidence in God. Go back and read the first two books of Nehemiah in the King James Version and Living Bible.

God has a way of showing us via his Word over and over again that He handles the impossible as he sees fit. Our job is to call on him and let him answer in his way and when he sees fit. What may be overwhelming and impossible to us is simple for God if we just call on him and trust him.

Praying is about having the right view of God and having absolute confidence. Either we believe in the attributes of God or we don't. God is omnipotent-all powerful. God is omniscient—all knowing. God is omnipresent—everywhere at the same time. I know this is even hard to fathom because we are finite but we must remember God is infinite.

This is why we pray. Now something else we should ask is why do we praise? Knowing the answer to this will help us. All through the Bible especially in the Psalms we are told to praise God. Take a look at Psalms 100; it's loaded with instructions to us to praise God: "1 Make a ioyful noise unto the Lord, all ye lands.

> "2 Serve the Lord with gladness: come before his presence with singing.
> "3 Know ye that the Lord he is God: it is he that hath made us, and not we ourselves; we are his people, and the sheep of his pasture.
> "4 Enter into his gates with thanksgiving, and into his courts with praise: be thankful unto him, and bless his name.
> "5 For the Lord is good; his mercy is everlasting; and his truth endureth to all generations."

Praise to God lifts our spirit from its troubles and helps us give our burden to the Lord. My last question is why do we hope? Because again the Word said we should put our hope in God. Webster said hope means a feeling of expectation and desire for a certain thing to happen. God wants us to have this hope in Him and His Word. He wants us to expect good. Please do not misconstrue this to mean "things." God is spiritual so we should expect many spiritual blessings. Stop looking for "stuff" alone.

We get so bothered and down when we don't get our "stuff; are you serious? God is so much more than "stuff." God helps us endure, God helps us get over, and God gives us strength. What kind of man is this who can give us hope in the midst of a storm? What kind of man is this who can calm our fears that are so legitimate? God can speak to our storm and say peace be still. Oh, when the storms of life are raging God wants us to say, Stand by me and He will be right there.

Our God is real, and when He says to pray, to praise and to have hope, we need to do that and expect the answer to come from him. The question is do you mind waiting? I don't know about you but I feel like the songwriter: My hope is built on nothing less.

1 My hope is built on nothing less
Than Jesus blood and righteousness;
I dare not trust the sweetest frame,
But wholly lean on Jesus's name.

On Christ, the solid Rock, I stand;
All other ground is sinking sand,
All other ground is sinking sand.

2 When darkness veils His lovely face,
I rest on His unchanging grace;
In every high and stormy gale,
My anchor holds within the veil.

Praise Him. Hallelujah.

God bless you,
Fwfm: nlw

Fear in Deep Trials

Let's talk about fear in certain situations. Your child is sick again and needs another operation. In your case the doctor has given you a negative prognosis in re cancer. Your spouse has said, "I want a divorce," and you never saw it coming and you had actually left your job for your family. How about just losing your job after purchasing a house six months prior? These are issues that cause legitimate fear because they are deep trials.

You know what the fear is; you don't know how the situation is going to work out and time is a factor. You need help and you need it now. You are scared you may lose everything. You didn't want these events to occur and you didn't see it coming. Now these unwanted circumstances are ever-present in your life. Sometimes the issues even compound with multiple problems hitting us all at once.

In most situations, it is only human to keep rehearsing in our mind; how did this happen? What could I have done differently? Well, suppose there is nothing you could have done? Fear or apprehension locks us up. We can't eat we can't sleep, and the unknown haunts us.

What can give us courage and comfort in times like these? Again we have to go back to the Scriptures. "13 For I the Lord thy God will hold thy right hand, saying unto thee, Fear not; I will help thee" (Isa. 41:13).

> 4 Rejoice in the Lord always: and again I say, Rejoice.
> 5 Let your moderation be known unto all men. The Lord is at hand.

⁶ Be careful for nothing; but in everything by prayer and supplication with thanksgiving let your requests be made known unto God.

⁷ And the peace of God, which passeth all understanding, shall keep your hearts and minds through Christ Jesus.

⁸ Finally, brethren, whatsoever things are true, whatsoever things are honest, whatsoever things are just, whatsoever things are pure, whatsoever things are lovely, whatsoever things are of good report; if there be any virtue, and if there be any praise, think on these things. (Phil. 4:4–8)

Listen, I understand we get in deep waters, this is not new. David is one of the people from Bible times who experienced the same feelings. In fact I'm going to give you some scriptures you will have to look up yourselves in 2 Samuel 21:15–22. Just when he thought it was over, David's soldiers had to fight with the giant Goliath's family bringing on more fear. Goliaths brother had David cornered for sure death.

David said this in the proceeding chapter in 2 Samuel 22:12–19, that it was as if God was saving him from the deep waters.

What God is trying to offer us is His unfailing presence and His peace in the midst of our storm. To the world it doesn't make sense because we can find hope and help in our time of need. God helps us with our fears even though they are ever-present. God reminds us we are not alone; He is with us all the way and will never leave us.

Despite the doctor's words, despite the loss of a marriage and despite a sick child or loss of a job, we must still lean on God. Let God speak to our heart. We have to turn from our troubles to Him. When someone says look your troubles in the face, NO! Don't do that, look God in the face and let God deal with your troubles.

When the devil comes to your door and you look via the peephole and see it's him, don't answer it; send Jesus to the door. Why open the door when you know it's trouble. Let Jesus handle it. Take your burden to the Lord and leave it there. In your deep waters let God speak to your storm and say "peace, be still."

Please hear me; we are never hopeless. That is what Satan wants us to feel. This is what the Word of God says about that in Habakkuk 3:16–19: "16 When I heard, my belly trembled; my lips quivered at the voice: rottenness entered into my bones, and I trembled in myself, that I might rest in the day of trouble: when he cometh up unto the people, he will invade them with his troops.

> "17 Although the fig tree shall not blossom, neither shall fruit be in the vines; the labour of the olive shall fail, and the fields shall yield no meat; the flock shall be cut off from the fold, and there shall be no herd in the stalls:
> "18 Yet I will rejoice in the Lord, I will joy in the God of my salvation.
> "19 The Lord God is my strength, and he will make my feet like hinds' feet, and he will make me to walk upon mine high places."

Yes, God knows what you are going through, what you are experiencing, and He is saying do not worry, this is not my first battle; lean on Me.

Our confidence and faith should never be in our circumstances, ability or even our resources, but in the goodness, greatness, and grace of God.

Therefore, when we are faced with difficult circumstances such as major illness, family crises, financial ruin, or other maladies, we must place our faith in God because He will be with us in everything we face. It is God's strength that will carry us through the deep waters/trials and take our fears away.

We must say, "Lord, this is beyond my control please be my strength."

God bless you,
Fwfm; nlw

Don't Worry

In this day and time, we worry about a lot of stuff and grant it there is plenty happening in our world. Nevertheless in comparison a whole lot was happening back then too in biblical days but God wanted us to keep in mind that no matter what happens He always has our best interest at heart. Satan would have us to believe God made us then left us here to fend for ourselves. We are quite familiar with that concept because so many of us are suffering from that with our own parents.

This is the reason it is so important to listen to God and not the devil. This is also the reason we should be reading the Word like it is food. God knew we would run into walls that seemed like they were impossible to climb. God also knew we would tunnel valleys that appeared endless. The question is did we read God's warnings and direction for times like these. Let's just go through some of them to encourage ourselves and get our footing again.

1. "Therefore I tell you, do not be anxious about your life, what you will eat or what you will drink, nor about your body, what you will put on. Is not life more than food and the body more than clothing? Look at the birds of the air: they neither sow nor reap nor gather into barns, and yet your heavenly Father feeds them. Are you not of more value than they? And which of you by being anxious can add a single hour to his span of life?" Matthew 6:25–27).

2. "Therefore do not be anxious about tomorrow, for tomorrow will be anxious for itself. Sufficient for the day is its own trouble." (Matthew 6:34)

3. "And which of you by being anxious can add a single hour to his span of life?" (Luke 12:25)

4. "Peace I leave with you; my peace I give to you. Not as the world gives do I give to you. Let not your hearts be troubled, neither let them be afraid." (John 14:27)

5. "Come to me, all who labor and are heavy laden, and I will give you rest. Take my yoke upon you, and learn from me, for I am gentle and lowly in heart, and you will find rest for your souls. For my yoke is easy, and my burden is light." (Matthew 11:28–30)

6. "Cast your burden on the LORD, and he will sustain you; he will never permit the righteous to be moved." (Psalm 55:22)

7. "Casting all your anxieties on him, because he cares for you." (1 Peter 5:7)

8. "Do not be anxious about anything, but in everything by prayer and supplication with thanksgiving let your requests be made known to God. And the peace of God, which surpasses all understanding, will guard your hearts and your minds in Christ Jesus." (Philippians 4:6–7)

9. But now thus says the LORD, he who created you, O Jacob, he who formed you, O Israel: "Fear not, for I have redeemed you; I have called you by name, you are mine. When you pass through the waters, I will be with you; and through the rivers, they shall not overwhelm you; when you walk through fire you shall not be burned, and the flame shall not consume you. For I am the LORD your God, the Holy One of Israel, your Savior. I give Egypt as your ransom, Cush and Seba in exchange for you." (Isaiah 43:1–3)

10. So we can confidently say, "The Lord is my helper; I will not fear, what can man do to me?" (Hebrews 13:6)

11. Trust in the LORD with all your heart, and do not lean on your own understanding. In all your ways acknowledge him, and he will make straight your paths. (Proverbs 3:5–6)

12. "No temptation has overtaken you that is not common to man. God is faithful, and he will not let you be tempted beyond your ability, but with the temptation he will also provide the way of escape, that you may be able to endure it." (1 Corinthians 10:13)
13. "What then shall we say to these things? if God is for us, who can be against us?" Romans 8:31)

That was just to name a few. I hope you were encouraged. Let me leave you with this thought from Corrie Ten Boom. Worry does not empty tomorrow of its sorrow. It empties today of its strength.

God bless you,
Fwfm; nlw

The Value of Stress

A family was out shopping one day and went into a potter's shack. The place was cramped as it was too small for all the people playing looky-loo. Eventually most of the crowd left, but one family decided to stay because their kids seemed interested in the pottery.

They noticed two shelves of finished vases, one on either side of the potter. With childlike innocence one of the kids reached out to touch a vase. The potter said, "Please don't touch the pottery on that shelf, you'll ruin it." Then in surprise to everyone he said, "Why don't you touch the ones on the other shelf?"

Of course everyone was curious why some vases could be touched but not others. Pointing to the "do not touch" shelf the potter explained, "These haven't been via the fire yet." You see there is more to making pottery than just making beautiful shapes and masterpieces out of blobs of clay. Once they are formed they have to bake at a certain temperature to make sure they hold their shape. If they get touched before the fire they are quickly marred and dented. Without the fire the vase is pretty, but it's fragile.

The other vases could be touched because they had twice been baked in his kiln at temperatures exceeding two thousand degrees. The heat makes the clay firm and strong. The fire makes the beauty last without being pushed out of shape (1 Pet. 1:6, 7).

Both Peter and this potter were talking to me about a fire that increases the value of something precious. There is a heat that burns, and another heat that beautifies. There is a God-produced, Father-filtered stress and then there is the world's stress. Overworked, too much on your schedule, not enough rest/recreation, no Bible reading or study, little prayer equals little power… You can't just keep spinning your wheel you wear out. You have to stop and take account.

God is trying to get us to (Ps. 34:14). He wants us to manage our stress via Him. The heat He brings will prove, strengthen, and beautify. Personal peace is not the elimination of stress it is the management of stress. If we live without pressure we become fragile as a potter's unfired vase.

God has skillfully reshaped us on His wheel, making a "big blob" into something beautiful, something valuable. The songwriter said, "Something beautiful, something good, all my confusion, He understood… What others had thrown away and considered refuse, God redeemed it and said, "You're beautiful."

We need to eliminate self-induced stress and allow the pressure of God to shape us and form us. If the pressure is taken off a piece of coal, there will be no diamond. Removing that irritating grain of sand from an oyster's tummy means having no pearl. Don't help a caterpillar in his struggle inside his cocoon; it is going via metamorphosis. If you remove the pressure/struggle you will doom him it to be a worm for the rest of its life.

The proper amount and proper kind of pressure or irritation and pain can be tools to develop. God may send a load, but He will never send an overload. The right pressure doesn't make you bitter it makes you better. The apple and peach tree and rose bush have to be cut by the pruning knife; yes the tree or bush looks hurt, but the result is sweeter and larger fruit and beautiful colorful roses.

Hebrews 12:7, 11

That's what we want, stress that contributes to peace. Good solid, hard training—no pain, no gain. When you know the end result is going to be made better it brings peace not undo pressure. It may still hurt, but you can handle it more calmly.

"God may move your earth but He won't give you an earthquake. God will let some snow fall on you, but it won't be an avalanche." (Phil. 4:7)

The devil wants to go beyond what God allows even using us to harm ourselves, but God "checks" him. God is trying to build us while Satan is trying to bury us. God will allow us to be pushed to the building point, but not to the breaking point. Only God knows the difference, and He filters every load of stress. I assure you (2 Cor. 12:9) grace…

God bless you,
Fwfm: nlw

One More Chance

How many times have we cried for one more chance? One more chance to get it right; one more chance to make it right with someone. One more chance to change. I know I can do better; I know I can be better; I know I can do it if you just give me one more chance. It all sounds so familiar doesn't it?

God has rebirthed us, realigned us, and recharged us; shouldn't we be a new creation by now? (1 Cor. 5:17). By now we should have come out of the darkness into the marvelous light. God is constantly calling us, seeking us. We cannot, we must not be comfortable in the darkness.

We ought to learn what pleases God and do that. Replace the darkness, don't be willingly ignorant. Light drives darkness away.

If we've asked for one more chance why are there pockets of darkness still in our lives? It's time to start judging ourselves as to whether we've truly been born again. Let me ask myself this question. Which do I love, "the light" or "the darkness"? If you truly want another chance then take advantage of it and make the necessary adjustments in your life so we don't have to continue this exercise.

Don't make God have to do like Mom when she came home earlier than expected and turned the lights on. There we are with whatever we're doing-busted for the entire world to see. Is this what you want God to do-turn the lights on in your life because you have simply refused to come out of the darkness? If you think God is not serious and doesn't give another chance, ask Jim Bakker, ask Jimmy Swaggart, and ask Haggard from Colorado.

Those who are caught in the dark because they refused to discipline themselves are embarrassed, shamed, and downright exposed.

Is that what you want, to have what you do in the darkness come to the light?

Listen, with all the time spent in the darkness, yes, the locust have eaten…but God can give us back more than that with another chance if we're serious. God will restore, He will redeem us.

God bless you,
Fwfm: nlw

Tension and Stress

"For we would not, brethren, have you ignorant of our trouble which came to us in Asia, that we were pressed out of measure, above strength, insomuch that we despaired even of life."
—(2 Cor. 1:8)

Please do not be swayed by the false prophets on TV. You shall have tribulation according to the Bible and it has nothing to do with the amount of faith you have. It's just the way of the world; it's the cosmos. Tension and stress are a part of our world now like air and water. All of us will be affected by it at some point. It is inherent for every human being Christian or otherwise.

The society in which we live is frenzied; for every walk of life it's different but still full of tension and stress for us all. Too many people are believing the garbage that pastors, Christians, missionaries, and such fare better than others exempted from the tension and stress. This is not true; where we fare better is we have the Holy Spirit to help us get through it. We have sort of a Sabbath-rest as children of God. (Don't get this twisted.)

The Word *tension* means "a state of being strained to stiffness, hence mental strain, and nervous anxiety with attending muscular stiffness. Stress is defined as "a force, acting on or within another thing, and tending to distort it, as by putting or twisting it." Together, they combine to produce inability to relax, mental strain, and muscular tenseness. Stress is excessive tension.

It's been said that hard work produces tension. No, good solid hard work can actually put the mind at rest and be quite healthy. More the wrong kind of work or too much work can be a contributory cause. Another cause is a lack of or inadequate spiritual resources. You have to have some spiritual capital to meet the heavy demands of the world. Without it you set yourself up for undo stress. (Read Psalm 40:10.)

Another cause is an attitude of anxiety. The habit of worrying about things beyond our control. This paralyzes us and sets up toxic tension. Then there is the condition of fear. Some folks are just afraid of every little thing. They get nervous, afraid, and it blocks their ability to function. Fear of new responsibility, untried tasks, physical fear in their body, and etc. Did you know all of this fear can affect the nervous system and even our spiritual life?

We can lose ability to sleep, which in turn makes us restless and irritable. We can't relax, we worry that God is not hearing our prayers, we're just a mess. Next we have a wrong attitude toward others. Where you harbor inner resentment against someone, it works havoc with the nervous system. We all know jealousy, envy, hatred, and all related vices are a cancer. They are not just soul destroying, they also reek serious damage on our health.

A bad attitude can cause serious tension and undo stress. It can even affect our eating habits (too much, too little). It affects our mind, we can't even think straight It's almost like time body and mind have formed an alliance against the spirit; of course this is going to have a negative effect.

So what do we do so that we are not taken into a stress/tension hostage or bondage situation? The first relief is to be perfectly honest with yourself. Do you want to resolve these issues? They are not going away on their own. Check your work schedule, is it too much? Have you actually forgiven others and moved on? How much quality time are you spending with God? Do you do any physical exercise, walking, running, swimming, weightlifting, dancing, and etc.?

Do you have a hobby like reading books, boating, hiking, and etc.? All of these type things renew the mind and open the avenues of your heart so your tension and stress can evaporate.

When you cleanse the mind, you automatically start a cleansing project with the heart. When these two are working together your spirit joins in with the three of these having a trifecta you can't help but feel and be better physically. (Read Matthew 11:28–30.)

God bless you,
Fwfmt: nlw

Serving

In order to give value to the Christianity we proclaim, we must give priority to the things that matter to God. Too many of us are choosing to become involved in things that pass away; things of the world. God insist that we choose that which has eternal value, but we rebel and make poor choices that haunt us.

If what you choose in life has no enduring significance then why are you choosing it? Did you read the part of the Bible that said to gain this whole world and lose your soul is unprofitable? If you want worthwhile living you first have to truly give yourself to Jesus. Secondly you have to allow yourself to be used by God to reach others; you must serve. Giving to others helps you appreciate what God has done for you.

This isn't something set aside for just ministers and missionaries; all believers are called to serve. We must share our faith via various means to those in need. Many times you don't have to go anywhere, you can serve God right where you are (Matt. 28:19). (Isa. 1:17, Gal. 6:2)

We really ought to get busy; there is so much work to be done. We should be saying like Isaiah: "Here am I Lord, send me." We need to be about our Father's business.

Be willing to do anything then we should seek God's specific plan for us. God has given each of us unique gifts and we should be willing to use them for His glory. Wherever we think we're coming up short the Spirit of God will overcome any limits we put on ourselves. A willing mind to serve is what is needed. God will empower you to do whatever He has called you to do. Through it all you end up helping yourself.

God bless,
Fwfm: nlw

Who Are We Fighting?

Our Lord is not so much interested in religion, but He is certainly invested in our life. The stained-glass windows, organ music, congregational hymns, and altar call prayers are okay but God is really more interested in loving marriages, good parents, love-filled homes, generous hearts, and believers who are willing to take a stand in the midst of a crooked and perverse generation.

To have folk today with undefiled minds and hearts is a blessing. To project God's truth and live His character in a sin-ridden world is a beautiful thing. We really only understand life when we see it from a biblical perspective. All of the nightly news, Internet and political news simply add to the illusion that we are working it all out.

That is a facade at best; the world as we know it is passing away. Our eyes and minds are constantly deceived by the distorted perspective, twisted beliefs, false values, and poor morals of a decaying world.

This is the very reason a lot of folk refuse to read the Bible; it sheds light on the truth. To know is to have to respond so people intentionally remain in the dark so they can carry on their deeds.

Of course it is deceiving ourselves but we still do it anyway. We cherry-pick God's Word for truths we want to hear. We have no intention of fully submitting; it's just too much to give up.

Our will is an executive agent and it just is not willing to submit to a higher authority (God), even when we know it is right to do so. Most of the time the struggle we are having in life is with ourselves. We don't want to say we do not agree with God's Word or we reject it but that is essentially what we are doing when we disobey it.

Life is a struggle; it is full of conflict and warfare. This is why we are so admonished by Paul in Eph 6:10–13: "¹⁰ Finally, my brethren, be strong in the Lord and in the power of His might. [11] Put on the whole armor of God, that you may be able to stand against the wiles of the devil.

> "[12] For we do not wrestle against flesh and blood, but against principalities, against powers, against the rulers of the darkness of this age, against spiritual hosts of wickedness in the heavenly places.
> "[13] Therefore take up the whole armor of God, that you may be able to withstand in the evil day, and having done all, to stand."

Life is not a bowl of cherries; it's more of a never ending wrestling match. Unless we submit ourselves to the judgment of God's Word and allow Him to inspire and encourage, lead, guide, and direct us, we are going to end up like everybody else.

Yes, make your plans in life. Enjoy yourself but honor and praise God; don't forget who created you. Too many of us have arrogance about us, where we are unbending, unchanging, and unyielding. We cannot be that way if we hope to succeed in this world. We have to submit to either God or Satan; go figure.

The grace of God can relieve our pressure and stress and give us victory. Without Him it is a sure defeat. We cannot complain how unfair life is when we already know what we are up against and choose to go it alone without God.

The main nature of our struggle is with ourselves and other people. Satan disguises himself via one form or another of the human race then assaults us via these people acting as agents or principalities, powers, rulers of darkness, and spiritual wickedness in high places.

The entire human race is under vicious assault. The devil is real, he is active and he is working day and night trying to subvert, undo, and defeat God's plan in human history. Behind the problems of the world, behind the evil that manifest itself in mankind, there is a hierarchy of evil spirits. It is the devil and his imps or fallen angels.

To avoid being caught up in the trap we have to reject the attractive lies of Satan and grab hold to the clear life giving truth of God's

Word. Never mind his disguises; we know what he is about. Second Corinthians 2:11: "[11] Lest Satan should get an advantage of us: for we are not ignorant of his devices."

Stop trying to say you didn't know. Stop saying my pastor didn't preach this. Second Timothy 2:15: "[15] Study to shew thyself approved unto God, a workman that needeth not to be ashamed, rightly dividing the word of truth."

This is a call to arms; we cannot wish Satan away. Put on your armor and fight. Please know 2 Corinthians 10:3–5: "For though we walk in the flesh, we do not war according to the flesh. For the weapons of our warfare are not carnal but mighty in God for pulling down strongholds, casting down arguments and every high thing that exalts itself against the knowledge of God, bringing every thought into captivity to the obedience of Christ."

> [10] Finally, my brethren, be strong in the Lord, and in the power of his might.
> [11] Put on the whole armour of God, that ye may be able to stand against the wiles of the devil.
> [12] For we wrestle not against flesh and blood, but against principalities, against powers, against the rulers of the darkness of this world, against spiritual wickedness in high places. (Eph. 6:10–12)

God bless you,
Fwfm; nlw

What You Working With?

You should know by now as a Christian you're in a war. We are engaged in spiritual warfare against Ephesians 6:12. It's beyond a battle, it's a campaign. This is not imaginary neither is it in the flesh, it's waged on an unnatural plane. It is not tangible; we cannot lay hands on these imps; only spiritual weapons will avail.

This mess all started when Satan was booted from heaven and ruined Adam and Eve in the Garden of Eden. Satan wields a vast amount of power unfortunately too little attention is paid to him. The Bible says we're not ignorant of his devices but we sure act like we are. As much as God tries to alert us we ignore Satan's insidious wiles; much to our demise.

There is a struggle between Satan and the church; accept it and get your weapons ready. Speaking of which, what are you working with? You will be persecuted, you will go through trials and tribulations, but if you follow the Word you will overcome (John 16:33).

How do you overcome Satan, via the Word and via faith (1 John 5:4, 5)? Four of Satan's names are dragon, serpent, devil and Satan. A dragon is a monster; you dread it. It is a sinister powerful beast, cruel, ferocious, and malicious.

A serpent is crafty, cunning, slippery, and works under guise or cover. It transforms itself into whatever it needs to so it can blend in and then attack.

The devil means slanderer. That is how the devil started out, slandering God to Eve and Adam. Then he slandered Job to God. Slander is one of the devil's most potent weapons; this is why he rejoices when children of God engage in this repulsive activity.

Satan means adversary of God and of the church, and the believer. He is the open enemy of all that is holy. Satan opposes all that is in man's highest interests or anything for God's glory. Not only so, he is an accuser of the brethren...

He is the father of lies. He accuses us to God and to one another (Job 1:7 KJV/The Message). Satan loves 415s or disputes with Christians and he has a highly organized hierarchy to carry out his sinister plots. So the question is what are we working with that helps us overcome him?

In order for Satan to hurt Jesus he attacks the brethren, many times right via the church itself. Believers attempting to discredit believers; what better way, a house divided against itself cannot stand.

So our no. 1 weapon our Lord and Savior or Commander in Chief wants us to use to engage in battle is His blood. That's right, the potency of the cross. It's not about us or our prowess; it's about our union with Christ in His death and resurrection. The "blood of the Lamb." This isn't a lucky charm or a rabbit's foot, it's an understanding of a relationship attesting our faith in the power of God.

Do you believe Jesus was born of a virgin? Do you believe He was raised from the dead? Well, this same "blood of the Lamb" activates our faith; it's the same Holy Ghost power. You want to bruise the serpents head as in Genesis 3:15 you do it via the "blood of the Lamb." Our victory is in the blood. By means "because of and every song writer picked up on it. 'What can wash away my sin...'"

"Oh, the blood done signed my name."

When we pray, plead the blood of Christ that shows we are firmly affixed on the victory of Jesus via the power of His resurrection.

Secondly, overcome by the word of your testimony. Live according to what you believe that Christ said and stand up. When you ground yourself in the Word of God and live accordingly you're speaking volumes to the world and Satan. This sort of testimony silences him and his emissaries. What a powerful testimony to stand on the Word and live it.

The Spirit of the Lord will give us wings as we continue to call on the name of Jesus. Our walk, our talk, and our actions will reflect Christ and His power. The next weapon is to love God and His Word more than you love anything else. You don't become a martyr but you realize you will take some hits from the devil but you affirm Christ is more powerful and you will overcome.

You die to self. You lose pride. You allow Christ to remake you; allow Him to sterilize or clean you and plant you as a seed to bring forth much fruit. That is your sacrifice, not your life per se but dedicating your very being to the kingdom of Christ. Live the Word, help people, be a living testimony in your marriage and family.

This is how the victory will come; these are tools you should be working with. You are undefeatable when you practice what you preach. "On Christ the solid rock I stand…"

Until Satan's judgment is executed and he is sent to Gehenna (hell fire) we must use our weapons of warfare because we will be called out again and again. Be a conqueror and a victor not a victim.

God bless you,
Fwfm: nlw

Waiting Ain't No Joke

With the way our society is set up waiting is not on the list; somehow, someway, we're expected to and are supposed to "make it happen." Well, just because our society is fast paced it doesn't mean our life has to be too.

The world tells us waiting is for losers; a passive acceptance of circumstances. They say it's a last resort, after we have failed to achieve what we set out to do. But the Word of the Lord clearly tells us "to wait on the Lord" (Ps. 27:14). It also teaches us that He will bless us greatly when we do (Isa. 64:4).

Now let's understand something, this type waiting does not imply idleness or apathy, but rather a determined stillness. It is a quiet, expectant, steadfast, courageous, and diligent activity that occurs when we slow down to receive further instructions.

Timeouts happen in sports and they should happen in our lives. It's a time to regroup, to rethink, and to re-strategize. The old way isn't working; let's take a time out to put together a new plan.

Even in battle timing is everything; timing and timeouts are very important. No, waiting ain't no joke. One of the main reasons we get in trouble in life is we run off without God; we become impatient, we get tired of waiting and we get out of God's timing.

Listen, when we actively wait, we place complete trust in Him whether or not we see results. Many times things are happening but we just can't see it. We don't need to become anxious, the Word has said over and over again that God has a divine plan for us; He has a reason for telling us to pause.

When we become impatient and take matters into our own hands, we step out of God's will. Now we're running interference and our failure to wait for the Lord is going to delay what God has set up for us. It delays our blessings and sometimes it even brings about pain and suffering.

The cost of not waiting on God can show up in relationships, finances, and many lost opportunities. Oh but when we are obedient and wait as God has instructed (Isa. 40:31) He gives us clear direction and we walk in step with Him—forward.

God uses this timeout or waiting period to prepare us for His will. It also strengthens our faith and sifts our motive. We desperately needed this timeout. Now we can get back in the game with renewed purpose.

God bless you,
Fwfm: nlw

Provision through the Trials

We make so many plans, many without God. I know we are advised against this but we trudge on anyhow. We choose a path that is so wrought with rocks until even our closest friends start to wonder. Why won't we listen to God's counsel so we don't collide with the rocks?

The prophet Habakkuk lived in a society just like ours today. Evil and corruption permeated the entire world including the so-called "believers." One would think with all the havoc Judah was brought through they would honor and obey God at every turn; yet it wasn't so. Selfish gain was their goal and just like in our time, corruption was everywhere.

There was a desperate need for the counsel of God. Godless ways were contaminating everything including the house of God. It got so bad until the Lord told Habakkuk the Babylonians would overwhelm them. Judah would be destroyed and in fact many children of Israel would be taken captive.

Habakkuk was so saddened by this news, he was also confused. Why would God allow a pagan nation to do this to Judah? Because they had long left God and were doing evil just like everyone else; However God didn't just abandon them. God used Babylonia as a tool to bring the nation back to himself (Hab. 1:12–17).

Yes, the Babylonians would be used to punish Judah for poor choices but then would also be dealt with. No one likes tough times of discipline or correction but many times God allows these sorts of issues for our ultimate good. Evil is all around us waiting to attack but God keeps it away via his angels. When we persist in going the wrong way God opens the flood gates and allows evil to chastise us.

Many of us don't believe it but repentance is needed, you can't keep choosing the wrong things without repercussions and consequences. God therefore told Habakkuk tell them I will deal with them but also tell them this. "⁴ Behold, his soul which is lifted up is not upright in him: but the just shall live by his faith" (Hab. 2:4, check NLV).

When we go via the vicissitudes of life whether our fault or not we have to have the right frame of mind. Habakkuk had that, which is why he was inspired by the Holy Spirit to write 3:17–19. "¹⁷Although the fig tree shall not blossom, neither shall fruit be in the vines; the labour of the olive shall fail, and the fields shall yield no meat; the flock shall be cut off from the fold, and there shall be no herd in the stalls:

> "¹⁸ Yet I will rejoice in the Lord, I will joy in the God of my salvation.
> "¹⁹ The Lord God is my strength, and he will make my feet like hinds' feet, and he will make me to walk upon mine high places. To the chief singer on my stringed instruments."

Look it up in NLV or The Message.

Habakkuk was able to tell the people the goodness of God and to offer thanksgiving in spite of the impending doom. God would see them through. God does not always move the mountains; sometimes He will use the mountains to make us stronger. God will help us tunnel through the mountains or walk the edges with hinds feet nimble like a deer.

Have you watched deer leap over dangerous crevices and go via terrain other animals freeze at? God produces in us a spiritual agility to climb where others might stumble and tumble down. Where many tremble in fear due to the size of the obstacle or difficulty we can be grateful to God as He makes us sure-footed.

Through the Holy Spirit we are safe and secure despite the treacherous peaks and valleys. We like Habakkuk can look forward despite our calamites with thanksgiving because we live by faith.

God can then use the very things and people who have caused us to stumble to be our stepping stones. God may not move our mountains but He sure gives us the strength to climb. That is provision via the trials.

God bless you,
Fwfm; nlw

Keep Yourselves in the Love of God

Jude 21 we have become so distracted today by so many things. The iPhone, TV, internet, movies, Netflix, politics, and so on. Not only have we been distracted, we have literally lost interest in God. As far as love for God we claim we have it but our actions show otherwise. It is sort of like a man saying I love you to his wife and kids but he is never home. Not only so he is seen with another woman whom he cannot answer why.

We have lost our love for God today. We have forgotten what He has done for us. We are too caught up in current events. Many of us are just hung up on our hang ups. We play our drama life over and over again until it gets the better of us. As many times as we think about it one would think we are rehearsing for a part in a movie.

We forget about Phil. 4:8; no we just keep looking in the rearview mirror. Woe is me... Have we forgotten it was God's grace that brought us safe thus far? Too concentrate on God is not easy it takes work. This is the reason Jude said, "keep yourselves in God's love." We cannot and we must not allow our problems to make us forget about all of what God has done for us. We have to keep remembering and building ourselves up in faith.

Every day we should be having family worship and private devotions. How often do we read the Bible? Most people have given up on family devotions. Most people have stopped reading the Word. They claim to still know God and love God but just don't want to talk about God unless there is a specific need like job loss or a death in the family.

Did you know that no association brings no relationship? The reason you can't win your family back is because you're never there. They never see you; they don't know you. They know who you are but they don't really have a relationship with you. It's apparent you love work or something else more than your spouse and children because you're never home. Let's just be real.

No excuses of I had to work. Why did you marry and have a family if you were not going to love them? Sixty-plus hours a week plus weekends; where is the love? Even if this crept up on us unawares (that happens) now that you know, what are you doing about it? Are you going to wait until you and the spouse are divorcing? Are you going to wait until you and your children are distant or until they are in trouble and don't trust you?

How about God? You haven't talked to Him on the regular either. Are you going to wait until you've lost your family, lost your job, lost your children? The Word says looking unto Jesus the Author and Finisher of our faith. I beseech you brethren; keep yourselves in the love of God.

How often do you pray? Do you pray for others? Do you ask for help from the Holy Spirit for direction? Do you even feel like you need help or guidance? You've just got it all down-pat, don't you?

My friend, this is God's will that you keep yourselves in love with Him. It's for your safety. It is a distinct special request that God is making of us. God knows the world, the flesh, and the devil are pulling at us. "Be sober, be vigilant; because your adversary the devil, as a roaring lion, walketh about, seeking whom he may devour. Come on. He expects us via the aid of the Holy Spirit to keep ourselves in love with Him" (1 Pet. 5:8).

May this work for you spiritually and in your family and in your personal life. Fight for the love of God; don't just give in to the cravings of the world. Don't just forsake God and family for some...

"Keep" yourselves; work out your soul salvation. Don't be lazy or lackadaisical. When it comes to God and your faith; it is too valuable to lose. Keep yourself in the love of God. Don't get caught up in stuff while you put God and family aside.

Don't let the fog of the world separate you. Stop allowing yourself to drift out to sea thinking everything is okay with God and family when obviously it is not. Come on now. [24]To him who is able to keep you from stumbling and to present you before his glorious presence without fault and with great joy—[25] to the only God our Savior be glory, majesty, power and authority, through Jesus Christ our Lord, before all ages, now and forevermore! Amen. How can God do this if you're busy doing your thing elsewhere?

God bless you,
Fwfm; nlw

Abiding in Him

Sometimes we can do some good and it can go to our head. Our humanness makes us think; hey I'm good, look what I can do. Well, please be reminded that anything you can do, God gave you the ability to do it. All praise and glory should go to Him. We cannot start boasting of our accomplishments when it's actually God working via us.

To make this a little clearer, we are the branches, Christ is the vine; we abide in Him. Without Him, we are dung. Think about it, how many times have you gotten in hoc and God's grace and mercy bailed you out?

Any fruit coming from us God produced it, so we cannot take the credit. Let's not try to impress others with our skills, let's be obedient to God and let Him use us for His purpose and glory.

We need to let the Holy Spirit live Christ via us. As long as we abide in Him (the Vine), we sap His strength. Our life should be spirit-filled; it should be exchanged for His life via us.

Galatians 2:20 says,

> "[20]I am crucified with Christ: nevertheless I live;
> yet not I, but Christ liveth in me: and the life
> which I now live in the flesh I live by the faith of
> the Son of God, who loved me, and gave himself
> for me."

So when you put it in this context we are just a branch. However we can't just hang there, we must at least have some leaves, flowers, or fruit showing that we are alive in Christ. Any fruit coming from us is not due to our effort, but due to our abiding in Him. Our roots are in Him; the more we surrender, the more He can fill us with His Spirit. That's how we abide in Him.

God bless you,
PS: When you get the chance Google John 15 to get a bet-
ter grip on the vine and branches understanding.
Fwfm: nlw

Lead Me, Cleanse Me, Fill Me

Part II

¹⁸⁻²¹ King David went in, took his place before God, and prayed: "Who am I, my Master God, and what is my family, that you have brought me to this place in life? But that's nothing compared to what's coming, for you've also spoken of my family far into the future, given me a glimpse into tomorrow, my Master God! What can I possibly say in the face of all this? You know me, Master God, just as I am. You've done all this not because of who I am but because of who you are—out of your very heart!—but you've let me in on it.

²²⁻²⁴ "This is what makes you so great, Master God!
There is none like you, no God but you, nothing to
compare with what we've heard with our own ears.
—2 Samuel 7:18–22

David is saying, God knows us and still loves us, wow!

You remember the Hosea love story? This is what God has done for us. God loved his people so much He sent Hosea to seek reconciliation with his unfaithful wife. She had abandoned him and the family again and returned to whoring, yet Hosea pursued her, and bought her back home. He didn't bring her home as a slave, but as a beloved wife. (Go ahead, Google it.)

This is what God did for Israel. This is what God did for us via Christ Jesus shed blood. I now beseech you, you must let God lead you, cleanse you, and fill you. Shouldn't we be humbling ourselves before God? Where is this pride and arrogance coming from?

Our heart should not be proud. Our eyes should not be lifted up and we should not be haughty. We should be like a mother's child crying for God to take us to His breast and feed us til we want no more.

We should be saying, "Oh, Lord, I praise you, I lift up your name; I magnify you. I long for your rescue and your leadership; your instructions are my delight. Oh, Lord, let me live so I can praise you."

We should be saying, "I've wandered far away from God, Lord I'm coming home…"

> [169] May my cry come before you, Lord;
> give me understanding according to your word.
> [170] May my supplication come before you; deliver me according to your promise.
> [171] May my lips overflow with praise, for you teach me your decrees.
> [172] May my tongue sing of your word, for all your commands are righteous.
> [173] May your hand be ready to help me, for I have chosen your precepts.
> [174] I long for your salvation, Lord, and your law gives me delight.
> [175] Let me live that I may praise you,
> and may your laws sustain me.
> [176] I have strayed like a lost sheep.
> Seek your servant,
> for I have not forgotten your commands. (Ps. 119:169–176, NIV)

There it is, in plain English, we just have to digest it and make it real in our life.

How about Psalm 51:7–9 (NIV): 7 Cleanse me with hyssop, and I will be clean; wash me, and I will be whiter than snow.

[8] Let me hear joy and gladness;
let the bones you have crushed rejoice.
[9] Hide your face from my sins
and blot out all my iniquity.

[13] And the publican, standing afar off, would
not lift up so much as his eyes unto heaven, but
smote upon his breast, saying, God be merciful
to me a sinner. (Luke 18:13, KJV)

This, my friend, is praying to be led. I would be remiss in my
ministerial duties to not give you this.

God bless you,
Fwfrn; nlw

Lead Me, Cleanse Me, Fill Me

This is a majority of the real problem so many of us have, we refuse to be led. We want to drive; we want to be in charge. Let God follow our lead. Are we even serious? Here's Jesus, this friend of sinners who came to seek and save the lost (Luke 19:10).

Here this true friend who loves us even when we do not deserve it. "8 But God demonstrates His own love toward us, in that while we were still sinners, Christ died for us" (Rom. 5:8). God looked for us when we were lost and had completely lost our way, is that a true friend or what?

Then 1 John 4:9: "9 In this was manifested the love of God toward us, because that God sent his only begotten Son into the world, that we might live through him."

But wait, it gets better; how about John 10:10: "10 The thief cometh not, but for to steal, and to kill, and to destroy: I am come that they might have life, and that they might have it more abundantly."

This is the God we serve. There is no greater friend or love than to lay down one's life for his friends (John 15:13). If we are going to call Jesus our friend and we can do that then we should understand friendship is a two-way street. What kind of friend are we to Jesus? Do we care about others? Do we help others? Are we mindful of the truth and do we do our best to live it?

Nothing has caused more pain to Christ than those who have said they know Him but have failed to prove it by their actions. Jesus said, "40 And the King shall answer and say unto them, Verily I say unto you, Inasmuch as ye have done it unto one of the least of these my brethren, ye have done it unto me" (Matt. 25:40).

Can we just be real; let us draw near to God He is our friend right? "8 Draw near to God and He will draw near to you. Cleanse your hands, you sinners; and purify your hearts, you double-minded" (James 4:8).

²² Let us draw near with a true heart in full assurance of faith, having our hearts sprinkled from an evil conscience, and our bodies washed with pure water.
²³ Let us hold fast the profession of our faith without wavering; (for he is faithful that promised;)
²⁴ And let us consider one another to provoke unto love and to good works:
²⁵ Not forsaking the assembling of ourselves together, as the manner of some is; but exhorting one another: and so much the more, as ye see the day approaching. (Heb. 10:22–25)

Is this asking too much from a friend?

Let us ask God to lead us, cleanse us, and fill us. We certainly do not want to be filled leaving the filth that is currently in us. We have to be cleansed, purged even, before considering being filled. To be anything otherwise why don't we just go outside and put whip cream on top of the trash or garbage in the can.

Does that sound gross and ridiculous? That is exactly how some of our lives are; trash/garbage with whip cream on top. There has been no change in us. Our hearts are stone and far from Jesus. We have not come to know Him and our actions prove it. Let's just be real for once.

Perhaps we should pray this prayer: "¹² But how can I ever know what sins are lurking in my heart? Cleanse me from these hidden faults. ¹³And keep me from deliberate wrongs; help me to stop doing them. Only then can I be free of guilt and innocent of some great crime.

"¹⁴ May my spoken words and unspoken thoughts
be pleasing even to you, O Lord my Rock and
my Redeemer" (Ps. 19:12–14, NLB).

In case you thought you could pull one over on God, He knows what we are really like. We may fool some of the people some of the time, but we can never fool God.

147

"[20] And what can David say more unto thee? for thou, Lord God, knowest thy servant." (2 Sam. 7:20, KJV)

"[11] The LORD knoweth the thoughts of man, that they are vanity." (Ps. 94:11)

"[9] The heart is deceitful above all things, and desperately wicked: who can know it?" (Jer. 17:9)

No friend of God, you cannot pull one over on Him; you would only be fooling yourself. This may even work for you for a while but its all vanity. Some folks are just wasting their time in church and playing religious because they will never see God; their heart is far from Him, you read the text.

If we really want to be led we should be praying these prayers. We should be reading, contemplating, and digesting God's Word. We should be asking God to deliver us from ourselves and the ways of the world. Too many of us are caught up.

We ought to see the holiness of God and be drawn toward it like a moth toward a flame.

[1] Blessed is the one
whose transgressions are forgiven, whose sins are covered.
[2] Blessed is the one
whose sin the Lord does not count against them
and in whose spirit is no deceit. (Ps. 32:1, 2)

This points us to being led, to being cleansed, and to being filled. Why do so many so-called Christians have so many problems? God in His grace and mercy has given us His Word and these prayers to lead us; to show us His way, now we must fall in line.

How great is our God? (More to follow.)

God bless you,
Fwfm; nlw

On Point with God

You are the storyteller of your own life; what are you writing? Is it fiction, nonfiction, science fiction, drama, what? We are supposed to be on a mission with God. We as believers are all commissioned to share our testimony/or life so someone else can live. Listen to this scripture and see what knowing God does to us and for us (Isa. 61:3): "³ To appoint unto them that mourn in Zion, to give unto them beauty for ashes, the oil of joy for mourning, the garment of praise for the spirit of heaviness; that they might be called trees of righteousness, the planting of the Lord, that he might be glorified."

You see even when we are counted down and out God helps us bounce back; we matter.

Are you doing what is important? Is it emphasized, is it recognized? Matthew 28:19 gave us some particular instructions to seek, save, and send the lost, are we doing that. It's not enough to come to church or Bible Study, we have to go out and share the truth. One preacher said it's like one beggar finding bread and telling the others where he found it.

> ¹⁹ Go ye therefore, and teach all nations, baptizing them in the name of the Father, and of the Son, and of the Holy Ghost.

We have to stop doing so much studying how to do it and just do it. We ought to seek out the lost with intention, purpose, passion, and focus. Can you imagine how many people would really be helped if all churches had an outward ministry instead of just coming to church or church meetings?

It should not be about what God can do for us, but what God can do through us. Can Jesus see your faith by what you do and how you live? Your feelings, your opinion, and etc. need to die to Christ so you can be born again to live for Him; you matter, get on point with God.

Now Peter and John went up together to the temple at the hour of prayer, the ninth hour. [2] And a certain man lame from his mother's womb was carried, whom they laid daily at the gate of the temple which is called beautiful, to ask alms from those who entered the temple:

> [3] who, seeing Peter and John about to go into the temple, asked for alms. [4] And fixing his eyes on him, with John, Peter said, "Look at us."[5] So he gave them his attention, expecting to receive something from them.
> [6] Then Peter said, "Silver and gold I do not have, but what I do have I give you: In the name of Jesus Christ of Nazareth, rise up and walk." [7] And he took him by the right hand and lifted him up, and immediately his feet and ankle bones received strength.
> [8] So he, leaping up, stood and walked and entered the temple with them—walking, leaping, and praising God. [9] And all the people saw him walking and praising God. [10] Then they knew that it was he who sat begging aims at the Beautiful Gate of the temple; and they were filled with wonder and amazement at what had happened to him.

The man from the beautiful gate (Acts 3:1–9) needed to learn how to walk as his bones were strengthened so he could walk. When you go, Jesus said I will be with you. The power or strength God has given you should be used to help someone or you will misuse it or it can turn into power to implode.

This is why some people turn on their family, God wants them to take their new found knowledge and zeal and reach out or outreach, but they instead become know-it-all and ruin their family. Don't allow yourself to get "backed-up" by taking too much in, but not let enough out. In a body this causes poison to build up.

Too many of us are just flexing in the mirror admiring how good we look (how much we know as Christians). No one is being helped; we're just staring at other Christians every Sunday, basically saying, "Don't I look good?" We are waiting for God to give us more power, and God is waiting for us to go so He can give us power.

Get on point with God and stop staring at you self. Deny yourself, take up your cross and follow God.

God bless,
Fwfm: nlw

Redemption

[15] Thou hast with thine arm redeemed thy people, the sons of Jacob and Joseph. Selah. [16] The waters saw thee, O God, the waters saw thee; they were afraid: the depths also were troubled. [17] The clouds poured out water: the skies sent out a sound: thine arrows also went abroad. [18] The voice of thy thunder was in the heaven: the lightning's lightened the world: the earth trembled and shook. [19] Your way was in the sea, Your path in the great waters, And Your footsteps were not known. [20] You led Your people like a flock by the hand of Moses and Aaron.

—Psalms 77:15–18

Our God is not only great, profound, and merciful but His sole concern is our redemption. God wants to buy us back from the sin that has consumed us in this cosmos (world) and restore us beyond salvation. That is what he did with Jacob and Joseph (v. 15). Then He uses the word Selah to show us this is a critical point; it means stop and think or pause and reflect.

To redeem means to restore to usefulness something that was rendered useless. EG typewriter to a pawnshop. Redemption is a special work that only God can do. No one else can redeem us from our sins. We can't even redeem ourselves. But our great God takes on this special project and everything He does in our life is focused on our redemption. On restoring us to usefulness for Him. Beyond our salvation God wants to make us Christlike to redeem others.

Do you know that many of the miracles in the Bible are redemptive in nature? Even what God did for the children of Israel from bondage to a place of usefulness for God in the land of promise.

The miracles that Jesus did in the Gospels-The transformation of water into wine, the healings and the feelings were all designed to impress people with truths that would transform their hearts and redeem their lives.

Of course the miracle of the resurrection was the most redemptive miracle of all for it was the supernatural event that made it possible for us to be saved from sin and death. In the crucifixion and resurrection God paid the ultimate price for our redemption. He bought us back from Satan's pawn shop and restored us.

The songwriter said, "Jesus saves…" (1 Cor. 8:9).

"For your sakes." (Isa. 53)

"At this very moment, Jesus is interceding for us in heaven" (Heb. 7:25, look them up).

V. 15 of Psalm 77 says, "With your mighty arm…"

Notice He didn't say that God redeemed the entire human race. Those who are God's people are redeemed. Those who are not God's people are not redeemed. Redemption is not just for everyone. No one was ever redeemed without their knowledge or against their will. Redemption is for those who respond to His invitation and act upon His Word.

The proclamation of God's redemptive love demands a response: Please don't be one of those who say "how can I know if God exist, I can't find Him so how can I believe? (Heb. 11:6). Draw near to God and He will draw near to you…

If you earnestly seek Him, you will find Him…

Are you one who is responding to God's redemptive call upon your life? Or are you sitting in sullenness waiting for God to do something for or to you in spite of yourself? (Verses 16–20, p. 77).

The psalmist now returns to that pivotal event the "Red Sea." What does he gather? First he recognized God's sovereign control over all the earth including nature. He observes that the waves of the Red Sea stood at attention as the commander in chief, God spoke to them.

Think about how the Israelites must have felt when they reached the edge of the Sea. The Egyptians were behind them and Mountains on either side. Their plight seemed hopeless. Yet the very thing that terrified them (the sea) was subject to God.

In the psalmist poetic imagery the water saw God and it writhed and convulsed in fear. God commanded Moses to stretch forth his staff. Moses obeyed and the sea parted. Wow! They were afraid of the waters, but the waters were afraid of God. The sea didn't dare touch these whom God was protecting with His mighty arm.

Remember, remember this is not the only time the waters had to bow down.

> [38] But He was in the stern, asleep on a pillow. And they awoke Him and said to Him, "Teacher, do You not care that we are perishing?"
> [39] Then He arose and rebuked the wind, and said to the sea, "Peace, be still!" And the wind ceased and there was a great calm. [40] But He said to them, "Why are you so fearful? How is it that you have no faith? [41] And they feared exceedingly, and said to one another, "Who can this be, that even the wind and the sea obey Him!" (Mk. 4:38–41)

There is something you and I can learn from this for the rough times ahead of fear and danger in our own lives. The very powers and forces that frighten us are themselves under the command of God. The thing you fear fears God. Forces of natures are nothing but instruments in God's hands.

Look at the psalmist verses in 17, 18 describing the elected storm; soul shaking thunder, lighting flashing across the heavens like fiery arrows. The earth trembling in response; all of these are under God's command. No power on earth, natural or human can operate except by permission of the almighty. This is what the Psalmist is trying to convey.

We know this is true as we see it illustrated in the last hours before Jesus went to the cross. Forsaken by His friends, betrayed by

Judas, and denied by Peter, Jesus stood alone and seemingly power-less before Pontius Pilate the Roman Governor. When Pilate tried to question Jesus, the Lord gave no answer. Frustrated Pilate asked, "[10] Then saith Pilate unto him, Speakest thou not unto me? knowest thou not that I have power to crucify thee, and have power to release thee? [11] Jesus answered, Thou couldest have no power at all against me, except it were given thee from above: therefore he that delivered me unto thee hath the greater sin" (John 19:10, 11).

Oh, how our lives would change if we truly lived by that great truth. God is the commander in chief. Every force, world system, authority, and etc., is under His sovereign control. The king's heart is in the hand of the Lord, as the rivers of water: he turneth it whith-ersoever he will.

"[2] Every way of a man is right in his own eyes: but
the Lord pondereth the hearts." (Prov. 21:1, 2)

We are only what God allows us to be; don't forget that.

All power in heaven and in earth is in His hands. Nothing can touch us without express permission of God Himself.

Verse 19 said God specifically led the steps of the Israelites via the depths of the sea. The children of Israel didn't know where God was leading them, but God had prepared the way. He knew what He was doing. As the psalmist ponders this miraculous event, he discov-ers a second great truth; the fact that we cannot understand what God is doing does not mean He is not at work in our lives.

I know this is a difficult concept for us to wrap our minds around. We are impatient beings and we want God to explain all of His plans and purposes to us right now. Well that is not going to happen. Unless God constantly reassures us we fret and panic just as the Israelites did when they reached the edge of the Red Sea.

Exodus 14 says the Israelites were camped in the desert near the sea when they saw a cloud of dust and heard the thunder of horses' hooves and chariot wheels. Pharaohs" army was coming after them.

The people cried out to the Lord… They panicked and blamed Moses for their peril in verses 11–12. The children of Israel lost faith in Moses and in God. We do the same when we lose a job, get divorced, or lose a loved one. Moses had to give them a pep talk in verse 13.

How can we criticize them when we would probably have acted in the same manner? Even today some of us whenever things go wrong and we cannot see the solution to our problems, we hit the panic button. Haven't you prayed in desperate situations, "Lord, there is no way out? I'm trapped. Why don't you do something?" This is not a prayer of faith, this is a prayer of panic and we all have prayed it at one time or another.

What the children of Israel didn't understand and could not imagine is that God had planned all along to lead them via the Red Sea. His path led right via the sea. His way led right via the mighty waters. God's plans of deliverance never even entered their minds; they wanted what they wanted.

Remember the old saying, "God works in mysterious ways and He is wonders to perform."

Though His footprints were unseen and His people were unable to understand His plan, God knew exactly what He was doing. His plan though hidden from the people was perfect.

This is a principle we need to put our minds around. Something we can rely on in those times when our back is against the wall, when our enemies are closing in or the obstacles in our lives seem insurmountable. When all hope is fading fast and there is no way out of total disaster, we need to place our confidence in Him who will not falter.

On Christ the solid rock I stand…

I know we cannot imagine what God will do, but we can trust that whatever He does it will be for our best as in Romans 8:28.

God has a way of erasing His footprints. You cannot see where He is coming from or where He is going but please know He has a plan (Jer. 29:11, 12). He led the Israelites out of certain death to safety and a far shore.

Have you ever been in a situation so desperate you could see no way out? You prayed and prayed but God seemed silent until finally He provided an answer from a completely unexpected source?

Sometimes we pray and God lifts us out of our affliction. Other times He leads us through our valley. In Israel's case God's path led via the sea, via the trouble via the trials. He didn't take them around it but right through it. You may not like God's method but the result is always for the best.

Finally, verse 20. God shepherds His people. Is there any description so eloquent and beautifully descriptive of a relationship of God to his people than that of a shepherd with his flock? It sounds just like Psalms 23.

Because the Lord is our shepherd we lack nothing; He supplies our needs… Meaning and purpose is an essential ingredient of life. Why are so many people depressed and suicidal today? Their lives lack meaning and purpose. Why are alcohol and drug abuse cases skyrocketing, even among the wealthy, successful and church people? They have no reason for living; they use chemicals to numb their pain and their meaningless existence.

A man once went to a counselor and he said listen, "I have everything I ever wanted, but I don't want anything I have." He was suffering from "destination sickness." The sickness of having achieved all of his life's goals only to find that none of his achievements brought him peace and satisfaction. What does it profit a man to gain the whole world and lose his soul?

Our great Shepherd of the sheep has redeemed us and given us meaning and purpose. He has given us a reason for living. He makes life worthwhile. He gives us love and everybody needs love. You need to know somebody cares; somebody is going to provide for you. You need to know somebody is going to protect you. First Peter 5:7 said it so well, "7 casting all your care upon Him, for He cares for you."

Our God, our Savior is the Good Shepherd as in John 10:11–15.

You don't have to ever feel abandoned or neglected. Our shepherd is on the job even when we are not aware. I don't know about you but I'm going to trust in the Lord until I die; Google the song.

God bless you,
Fwfm; nlw

Constant Conversion

We've all been to weddings and heard the bride and groom say, "I do." Before that they pledged their love for each other. Before that they told each other "I love you" many times. Do you know why there is all of this redundancy, or repeatedness? It's because it is reassuring, that's why. Nobody wants to hear I love you once, and it's never repeated again. For that to happen, it makes you question whether or not it was real when you initially heard it.

Well, I was just making a point here, we're not really going to talk about love, we're going to discuss conversion. The songwriter said, "I came to Jesus as I was; I was weary worn and sad. I found in Him a resting place and He has made me glad." Okay, what have you done since?

Have you shown that your conversion was real by how you live? Have you changed for the better? Have you become a new creation as in (2 Cor. 5:17). Have you been transformed by the renewing of your mind…as in Romans 12:1, 2. So what I'm getting at is have you continuously grown in your Christianity showing that your conversion was authentic?

Let me be clear on something here, we only need to be saved once, but we need a continuous conversion. There are parts of us that need constant cleansing. One little rinse a few years ago is not going to cut it. We have to be constantly, steadily and continuously cleansed or converted all the days of our lives.

Just like you raise a child from one to twelve, then monitor what you've raised from thirteen to eighteen, you're still not done. They still need help, maybe even more now. They need continuous help all through adulthood, all through their life.

We too must turn to God as children like it says in Matthew 18:3. We are dependent upon Him; He is our Father. We cannot be left to our wits as if we've made it now. We will err again and again and we should be corrected again and again. To make the process simpler, we should confess again and again (1 John 1:9).

We are responsible for our growth or lack thereof. Either we want to continuously grow up in God or be retarded (slow growth). Don't we have enough retarded (slow growth) Christians? We need to fully give up to Jesus, and this is not going to happen at our initial conversion. It takes repeated conversions, continuous conversion. Why, because the longer we're on this earth, the stronger our will becomes. Our will is the opposite of God's; it has to be taught to submit or heel because it is stubborn or obstinate. It takes time to fully convert, just like it takes time to fall deeply in love and commitment.

It must be repeated again and again to sink in. We cannot allow our "old man" to dictate to our "new man." The "old man" must be mortified according to the Word (Rom. 8:13). The "old man" is a hindrance. The whole attempt of the "old man" is to block growth of "the new man." Do you leave your spouse's ex-wife or ex-husband with them alone; of course you don't because you don't trust their motives.

Do not let your pride keep you from being continuously converted. Just like in a marriage, there are whole areas of your life that have not yet been turned over. You don't just become Mrs. Jones forgetting your maiden name or life. Neither do you become Mrs. Christian forgetting your old life. It calls you, but you must ignore it and not allow it to get your attention. You must be continuously converted to Mrs. Jones or Mrs. Christian. Should you think like this you will steadily grow to become what God would have you to be and a good husband or wife too.

God bless you,
Fwfm: nlw

159

That's a Shame

Adam and Eve chose sin over innocence. They made a choice, a bad choice. Their eyes were opened and they were so filled with shame that they hid from God. Shame is like that; it is destructive. Shame keeps us from communicating with an outside world that can help us. Shame makes us think we are beyond help.

In actuality, we really don't want to face up to what we have done so we hide behind shame. We either don't know or don't care that God's grace is sufficient and will handle our malfeasance. God will forgive us and give us a new slate but we have to forgive ourselves.

We must let grace do its perfect work. Whatever we have done it is fixable. God is like the detergent Shout Out; a powerful stain remover. When other detergents did not work, one touch of God and our stains are gone.

Yes, there are consequences for sin but that doesn't preclude forgiveness. We cannot trap ourselves in a prison of self-condemnation after the grace of God sets us free. Who are we to say we feel unusable or dirty, or like trash when God has said we have become new? Why have we become a prisoner in our thoughts and heart when God has set us free?

Are we not paralyzing ourselves due to shame? Forget what you heard or what you feel and go by the Word.

> "⁹ If we confess our sins, he is faithful and just to forgive us our sins, and to cleanse us from all unrighteousness." (1 John 1:9)
> "⁷ Purge me with hyssop, and I shall be clean: wash me, and I shall be whiter than snow." (Ps. 51:7)
> "¹⁰ He hath not dealt with us after our sins; nor rewarded us according to our iniquities.

"[11] For as the heaven is high above the earth, so great is his mercy toward them that fear him.

"[12] As far as the east is from the west, so far hath he removed our transgressions from us." (Ps. 103:10–12)

"There is therefore now no condemnation to them which are in Christ Jesus, who walk not after the flesh, but after the Spirit." (Rom. 8:1)

"[17] Therefore if any man be in Christ, he is a new creature: old things are passed away; behold, all things are become new." (1 Cor. 5:17)

So you heard it straight from the Word now knock off the shame technique. We must stop carrying burdens God has already relieved us of. This is a tool of the devil so there can be no reconciliation.

Jesus calls us to his grace. He calls us out of darkness into the marvelous light. He calls us out of shame and degradation to freedom. No more sin bondage, no more crippling due to our past. He has forgiven us and cast our sins as far as the east is from the west. Why are we now saddling up with undo weights?

God forgives us, God cleanses us, God rescues us, now why let shame impede our progress? Grace is powerful, why cheapen it with restrictions? God lifts bowed down heads. God heals broken hearts; we just have to give God a chance.

Adam and Eve had to do it and we have to do it. We made the error now we have to make the move to allow God back into our lives. Moving closer to God will always require us moving away from something or someone else. If you have to leave someone or something behind so be it; it's them or God; choose right. Walk away from people or a habit or addiction; whatever is keeping you from God.

Sometimes we have to remember the Word literally; all things are lawful for me but all things are not expedient. Just because I can doesn't mean I should. Just because it's not illegal doesn't make it okay. If it hampers me I need to let it go. This may mean what we watch, where we go, who we hang with; whatever deters our relationship with God should be curtailed.

Adam and Eve learned this the hard way, must we follow suit? They had it all and forsook it to follow after what was hollow. They paid a great price too. We must choose better and break away from the norm. We must keep in mind that God wants to transform us; that is difficult if we insist on doing our own thing.

Then when we get caught doing our own thing we refuse to kneel due to shame (Jer. 6:15). "Were they ashamed when they had committed abomination? Nay, they were not at all ashamed, neither could they blush. Therefore they shall fall among them that fall; at the time that I visit them they shall be cast down," saith the Lord.

God is asking each of us where we are; we need to stop hiding and respond to Him. No more wandering, no more getting lost in the cracks and crevices. Forget the shame and surrender. God is sure to take us to new heights. Listen to this song:

> I've wandered far away from God,
> Now I'm coming home;
> The paths of sin too long I've trod,
> Lord, I'm coming home. Coming home, coming
> home,
> Nevermore to roam;
> Open wide Thine arms of love;
> Lord, I'm coming home.

> 2
> I've wasted many precious years,
> Now I'm coming home;
> I now repent with bitter tears,
> Lord, I'm coming home.

> 3
> I'm tired of sin and straying, Lord,
> Now I'm coming home;
> I'll trust Thy love, believe Thy word;
> Lord, I'm coming home.

4

My soul is sick, my heart is sore,
Now I'm coming home;
My strength renew, my hope restore:
Lord, I'm coming home.

5

My only hope, my only plea,
Now I'm coming home;
That Jesus died, and died for me; Lord, I'm coming home.

6

I need His cleansing blood, I know, Now I'm coming home;
O wash me whiter than the snow; Lord, I'm coming home.

God bless you,
Come home
Fwfm; nlw

Who Are You?

I wanted to be blunt in this question because too many of us struggle with identity crises. We don't know who we are or what we have become. We struggle in our regular life and we struggle in our spiritual life. How can we live to our maximum if we don't even know who we are?

Many of us are so easily defeated because we give in to temptations and sinful habits. The issues overwhelm us and before we know it we are somebody or something unrecognizable.

It is important to know yourself. Know thine own self. It is also important to know who we are in Christ. According to 2 Corinthians 5:17: [17] Therefore if any man be in Christ, he is a new creature: old things are passed away; behold, all things are become new. Has this happened with us or have we reverted back to old ways and old habits?

We ought to feel born again. We ought to feel there is a newness about us. The Bible keeps talking about a new living way; have we found it? Does our life show we are on that road?

Something that may be confusing but need not be and that is our old nature (who we were) can never be reformed or renewed. This is the reason Jesus said we must be born again or made anew (John 3:3–6).

We were born in sin and shaped in iniquity. We were set free from that bondage by accepting Christ redeeming blood. Basically we have had a blood transfusion. Christ indwelling Spirit has set us free.

We now have a renewed mind and we have laid aside the old self (Eph 4:22–24): 22 That ye put off concerning the former conversation the old man, which is corrupt according to the deceitful lusts;

> [23] And be renewed in the spirit of your mind;
> [24] And that ye put on the new man, which after God is created in righteousness and true holiness.

Our whole way of living now is different from the world. We walk differently, we talk differently, we even sing differently. Our desires are different, we even know how to be angry and sin not. We practice not letting the sun go down on our wrath. It isn't so much us as the Spirit of the Lord in us.

We have put on the Lord Jesus Christ and we make no more provision for the flesh (Rom 13:14). We now practice holiness, compassion, kindness, humility, gentleness, patience forgiveness, love and peace. This is who we are now.

God bless you,
Fwfm; nlw

Defragmentation

I'm not all that computer literate but I do know sometimes my computer is very slow and dragging. Come to find out there is a reason for this sluggishness. Apparently after much use with numerous programs and documents it causes pieces of information to become scattered. The computer then has to search for the pieces before it goes on to its next function. To fix this slowdown or sluggishness you have to run a program that retrieves the pieces and groups them together where they are easily accessible. This process is called "defragmentation."

Just like our computer, our lives also get fragmented. From relationships, jobs, family, finances, one situation tugs on our emotions while we are trying to concentrate on something else. Demands from every direction bombard us. We want to accomplish everything that needs to be done, but our mind won't settle on one thing long enough; it just keeps jumping around.

Of course if the mind can't settle, neither can the heart or body. It's not long before we begin to feel weary and useless and start slowing down. It's almost like what David said in Psalms 55:1–8. I'm going to give it to you in The Message you can look at it later in KJV or NIV: [1-3] Open your ears, God, to my prayer; don't pretend you don't hear me knocking. Come close and whisper your answer.

> I really need you. I shudder at the mean voice,
> quail before the evil eye,
> As they pile on the guilt, stockpile angry slander.
>
> [4-8] My insides are turned inside out; specters of
> death have me down.

I shake with fear, I shudder from head to foot.

"Who will give me wings," I ask—"wings like a
dove?"
Get me out of here on dove wings; I want some
peace and quiet.
I want a walk in the country; I want a cabin in
the woods.
I'm desperate for a change from rage and stormy
weather.

Lord, I'm scattered, restless, and only half here. It's going to take some serious prayer to defragment our lives. When we cast our care upon Him, He will sustain us (Ps. 55:22).

We actually need prayer the most when we have the least time to pray. This will help greatly in our defragmentation. We must remember (Ps. 55:22).

God bless you,
Fwfm: nlw

Praise Our Great God

Dogs staying with their owner in the woods, in the cold; laying on them to keep them warm. Dogs running and barking to alarm anyone that their owner is hurt or fallen and can't get up. How wonderful and loyal dogs are. Why do they do it, because they love their owner.

Love prompts action. Just like when God saw us trapped in sin He sent His only begotten Son to die for us to restore our relationship with Him. Love makes one act on behalf of the one you love. Here is something else love does in re the Lord. It tells us that as we delight in the Lord He awakens desires within us that reflect His heart.

Psalm 37:4 says it well: [4] Delight yourself also in the Lord, And He shall give you the desires of your heart. When one has true faith, true love and true praise it causes us to act. More than our emotions get in gear. We get challenged by our feelings to leave the old way and all things become new. [17] Therefore if any man be in Christ, he is a new creature: old things are passed away; behold, all things are become new (2 Cor. 5:17).

We begin to reach for something beyond ourselves in praise to our God. Did you know praising God does not come natural? No, our natural tendency is to just kick it, have fun, and satisfy our flesh. The Spirit of the Lord moves us to love Him, to praise Him.

Our "self struggles, but the love of God wins out and we find ourselves praising God even in difficult times and situations (1 Thess. 5:16–18).

[16] Rejoice evermore.

[17] Pray without ceasing.

[18] In every thing give thanks: for this is the will of God in Christ Jesus concerning you.

We start delighting in the Lord beyond feeling it, we want to live right, give right, do right, walk right, talk right, and etc.

You see the Word moves us to praise Him; that is what all the fuss is about. We delight in Him as Psalm 37:4 says because He is alive in us and we to Him. The Spirit calls us, He beckons us.

Real praise cost us something too. It changes our whole way of thinking. It doesn't end singing a song, or clapping our hands or going to church. That is just the beginning. It changes our whole way of thinking, living and being. We treat people differently in praise to God.

You know when you're really praising God rather than just giving lip service because real praise moves us. It moves us not to shake and dance or say Amen. It moves us to act; to praise God; to draw near to Him in how we live and to abandon sin and embrace His Word in every aspect.

We really start to become more like Christ when we praise Him according to His Word. If you don't see emphatic changes, guess what, you're not praising Him, you're marking time. (Google the song "More Love To Thee O Christ.")

You're going to church, singing in the choir and it has no effect on how you live. Are you even listening to the Word? You cannot meet God and stay the same. If you are not changing, sorry—you are not praising. You are marking time; you're lip synching. So many people do this until they really believe they are praising God.

What does God say about it? Take a gander at what Joel 5:21–24 says.

[21] "I hate, I despise your feast days,
And I do not savor your sacred assemblies.

[22] Though you offer Me burnt offerings and your
grain offerings,
I will not accept them,
Nor will I regard your fattened peace offerings.
[23] Take away from Me the noise of your songs,
For I will not hear the melody of your stringed
instruments.
[24] But let justice run down like water,
And righteousness like a mighty stream.

God is tired of hypocrites He wants a changed heart and changed lives. If you know Him you ought to have some of His characteristics. You certainly have some of your mom and dad's character; why not God's?

When you delight in God, in God's Word, it moves you; you become a part of it. It prompts you, it beckons you, and it woos you. If you still willfully sin and treat others with disdain perhaps you should monitor yourself. Do you really believe you are praising God? Judge yourself… Old folks say "empty wagons make a lot of noise." Go figure.

True praise challenges us to walk away from the past to a better place. The human heart is deceptive and wicked; it makes you believe you are in love with someone or something when all is infatuation—empty lust.

Real love moves us, it is a verb, we become. God's Word calls us to a higher way of thinking. A higher way of thinking causes us to act differently. God never leaves us where we are or where He found us.

This is what James 4:8 says, [8] Draw near to God and He will draw near to you.

Cleanse your hands, you sinners; and purify your hearts, you double-minded. The power of God can change anybody. Be leery of people who just keep talking about God and singing about God and lifting their hands in alleged praise. When the Spirit of the Lord moves they ought to change. Water was parted, light came into darkness, blind people received sight, deaf people began to hear and the dead were raised. All of this by the Holy Spirit, but you're still the same—go figure.

You're telling me you are praising the same God I am praising yet you are still caught up in the same sin traps? So God can raise the dead, but you can just give him ineffective lip service praise with no change in your life—thereby showing empty praise from an empty person. Again, do you really believe this; do you really believe you're praising, have you read the Word?

Why don't you face the truth? Nothing is too hard for God. If you haven't changed yet you believe you're praising Him, perhaps you really don't even know him. (Google Matthew 7:21–24.)

Knowing God compels us to love others (all) not judge them. We help those without; we don't single them out by percentage and label them as lazy and good for nothing. Jesus said when you've done it unto the least of these you have done it unto me. I'm going to stop here because this is really turning into a sermon now.

May all praise and glory be to God starting with my life changing and causing me to become more like Christ. We have been rescued by the holiness and righteousness of God; it ought to show in everything we do and say. That is real praise.

Praise God from whom all blessing flow. Praise Him all creatures here below. Praise Him above ye heavenly host. Praise Father, Son, and Holy Ghost.

Thank you, God, for rescuing me from me, this world and Satan. Let me now reach out to others in outreach and pick them up out of the mire. That's praise.

God bless you,
Fwfm; nlw

I Want a Clear Conscience

What is a conscience? According to Webster it is a special activity of the intellect and emotions that enables one to judge between good and evil also to perceive moral distinctions. Someone else described it as the testimony and judgment of the soul giving approval or disdain for certain acts. So we have gathered that for the most part conscience is the activity of our mind that makes us culpable of sin.

Continuing with legal terms like culpability, conscience is the nerve center or the soul, sensitive to moral pleasure and pain. Its function is to adjudicate on the moral quality of our actions and how we should act in view of it.

To ignore this very conscious function of our being, this healthy God given exercise is to ask for serious spiritual and emotional disorders. Having a conscience keeps us sane or okay. This is the reason so many people limp through life because they ignore their conscience and get into serious peril.

If your own conscience is being ignored, why should you listen to others? After a while you're a loose goose, doing whatever you please. You have to apprehend your conscience and appropriate its faculties, lest you suffer needlessly.

The conscience is the power to hear the voice of God in the soul. It is the highest and most mysterious faculty in the moral nature of man and it speaks with convincing authority when habitually obeyed. When we obey it, it speaks volumes.

When we do wrong it turns round and round in us and hurts very much. If we keep doing wrong it will turn so much the corners become worn off and it doesn't hurt anymore. We end up with a seared conscience. A conscience without feelings because it has been abused and ignored way too many times.

Please note that the conscience is not an executive faculty. It has no power to make a person do right or cease doing wrong. It merely or simply delivers its judgment. It produces the appropriate emotion then leaves it to the mind and will (which do have executive powers).

Look at Romans 2:15: [15] Who show the work of the law written in their hearts, their conscience also bearing witness, and between themselves their thoughts accusing or else excusing them.

You see the mind and will are the administration of the body. You will do what they say. You will act accordingly. They have the final verdict to the body's actions. Beyond that the conscience has no further responsibility. Our conscience witnesses our moral standard or lack thereof and testifies, to what it has observed.

Now here is a little play on words. Every conscience needs instruction so it can adjudicate accordingly. If this delicate mechanism has been thrown off balance their judgment will be off balance also. In man's case we are already behind the eight-ball because our conscience was thrown off balance in the fall of Adam and Eve (mankind).

In order to be reconnected or re-aligned, or corrected with proper moral judgment we need the WORD. The Living Word (Jesus). The Written Word (Bible), and the spoken Word (preaching). The Word will set us straight but we first have to heed it.

The Word will regulate the conscience and monitor the soul. The Word will insist on doing right and condemn wrong. The Word will produce remorse rather than unconfessed sin fanned around. The Word will impart peace to our soul.

You can read the whole portion of Acts 24:10–16, but here is v. 16: [16] This being so, I myself always strive to have a conscience without offense toward God and men.

Conscience is big my friend. This is the reason there are so many mixed UP, confused, emotionally ill people walking around, even in the church. You have to come clean. The human body cannot carry this kind of weight.

Too many people have told their conscience to take a hike and their conscience said okay if that is what you want. I'll go, but I'm taking sanity with me. We said "just go, I don't care." Conscience then said, "Okay, but you'll be sorry."

If your conscience is weak and vacillates like a compass with a weak magnetic current you are going to end up lost in the woods because you allowed your conscience to be too easily influenced.

How do you recognize a weak conscience?

1. Imperfect knowledge of God's Word and will.
2. Imperfect or weak faith or un-surrendered will that vacillates in its choices.

Listen anyone who obeys God's revealed will or is willing to do what is right is not harassed by an over-scrupulous conscience. They can function normally without seemingly being confused and being overly emotional. When you see people acting overly emotional they are wrestling with their conscience.

A defiled or weak conscience is a dangerous thing. They will do almost anything. There is no mind police. The conscience was an agent and it was ignored. To persist in some action our conscience has condemned or protested is to defile our conscience and pervert its faithful action or function. You just put a monkey wrench in the mechanism.

Titus 1:15: 15 To the pure, all things are pure, but to the defiled and unbelieving, nothing is pure; but both their minds and their consciences are defiled.

I'm trying to help somebody here.

An evil or guilty conscience results from habitual defilement. Hebrews 10:22: 22 Let us draw near with a true heart in full assurance of faith, having our hearts sprinkled from an evil conscience, and our bodies washed with pure water.

If the one who possesses such a conscience continues to practice evil then it will permit him or her to do it with less impunity (guilt or blame). It lowers their standards until it goes to regard evil as good and good as evil.

"20 Woe unto them that call evil good, and good evil; that put darkness for light, and light for

174

darkness; that put bitter for sweet, and sweet for bitter!" (Isa. 5:20)

I know you say a lot of people do this, yes and a lot of people will eventually fall hard too. You see, this my friend is a seared conscience. It is the ultimate condition of one who has habitually defied reason. It is to their own demise. The conscience is now reduced to insensitivity and no longer protests.

"2 speaking lies in hypocrisy, having their own conscience seared with a hot iron, Can I make it any clearer? We must stop rationalizing, excusing, and justifying our actions: wrong is wrong. You can't make a red-light green or yellow." (1 Tim. 4:2)

You can appeal it to your conscience all you want it is to no avail. This is what Alexander Pope said: Vice is a monster of such that to be hated, needs frightful men to be seen. Then seen too much of. familiar with her face we first endure, then pity, then embrace. Wow!

Did you not see the downward progression? Weak then defiled or seared. It will then become menacing if not cleansed or purified. It deteriorates, it must be restored, and renounced or else...

It has become evil and permissive. Listen to this; "My conscience did not bother me." Did you ever think that ultimately your conscience was seared? Conscience is kept pure and sensitive as we obey the light shed on our conduct by the scriptures.

You want to know how the church got messed up; violating the scriptures. Look at this:

> 8 Likewise deacons must be reverent, not double-tongued, not given to much wine, not greedy for money, 9 holding the mystery of the faith with a pure conscience.10 But let these also first be tested; then let them serve as deacons, being found blameless. (1 Tim. 3:8–10)

Yep, officials in the church left the Word and their conscience left them. They still believe they are right despite the demise of the church. Will anybody stand up for what is right? "5 But the goal of our instruction is love from a pure heart and a good conscience and a sincere faith" (1 Tim. 1:5).

People who love God love instruction. Instruction saves. Its reproof is welcomed and acted on by eliminating what is wrong and adding what is deficient. This brings serenity and heart rest. This brings peace of mind. Can you imagine all your urine and bowel refusing to leave your body? Yeah, instant poison to the body; that's what I'm talking about.

It's one thing for the world to be in turmoil; what's wrong with the church? Bad consciences. "7 Having therefore these promises, dearly beloved, let us cleanse ourselves from all filthiness of the flesh and spirit, perfecting holiness in the fear of God. This is where we should be but where are we really?" (2 Cor. 7:1).

Let us take the executive administration of our bodies the mind and will and make a definite act and purge the bad and add the good. Let us do this as led by the Holy Spirit. Let us separate ourselves from all we know to be sinful and contrary to God's will. To be unwilling to do this is to disqualify ourselves from experiencing the cleansing from the blood of Jesus Christ.

> 7 But into the second went the high priest alone once every year, not without blood, which he offered for himself, and for the errors of the people:
> 8 The Holy Ghost this signifying, that the way into the holiest of all was not yet made manifest, while as the first tabernacle was yet standing:
> 9 Which was a figure for the time then present, in which were offered both gifts and sacrifices, that could not make him that did the service perfect, as pertaining to the
> conscience:
> 10 Which stood only in meats and drinks, and divers washings, and carnal ordinances, imposed on them until the time of reformation.

[11] But Christ being come an high priest of good things to come, by a greater and more perfect tabernacle, not made with hands, that is to say, not of this building;

[12] Neither by the blood of goats and calves, but by his own blood he entered in once into the holy place, having obtained eternal redemption for us.

[13] For if the blood of bulls and of goats, and the ashes of an heifer sprinkling the unclean, sanctifieth to the purifying of the flesh:

[14] How much more shall the blood of Christ, who through the eternal Spirit offered himself without spot to God, purge your conscience from dead works to serve the living God? (Heb. 9:7–14)

Yeah, it just got real…

Let us use the available sacrifice and personally appropriate it.

The spring water can run fresh again now that we have removed all the standing water, algae, debris, and impurities.

God bless you,
Fwfm; nlw

What's Next?

When one looks at the Bible, we find a sort of pattern. God takes nothing and makes something and it is good. Over and over again God does this until we think we understand. Suddenly unpredictably things change.

Adam and Eve get kicked out of the garden. Cain kills Abel. Man starts to become self-absorbed loving things and himself more than God. It became so bad until God regretted that he even made man (Gen. 6:6).

It makes one wonder what's next? No one knows, there is much speculation but no one really knows what is next. Sort of reminds you of our lives today doesn't it? Things can be going well then out of the clear blue you lose your job. Your marriage suffers a major blow and disintegrates. Family relationships follow and go down the toilet. Sister and brother, aunts and cousins fight intensely to the point where you wonder how could there even be a relationship.

Then we lose a loved one or two followed by our beloved pets. We are messed up emotionally, we are broken. Next our health starts to fail. It makes us wonder, wow, what's next? What happened to our stability that we felt was so secure?

Now we are just waiting on God with all hope in his deliverance. We have fallen into the same pattern as the Bible; no one knows what to expect. No matter what anyone says, the ways of God cannot be predicted.

At best what we can do is stay in constant prayer or communication with God and hold his Word to our heart. He is the light to our pathway and the lamp to our feet. We and this world are fragile so don't be fooled into thinking you are strong. God is the strong one; we are living off of his strength. We need to trust him. Nothing in this world lasts.

It's all going by the wayside but our God is eternal. One day we will be with him but we don't know when. What's next, we don't know but God does. This is why the songwriter wrote the song "I Don't Know About Tomorrow"... Really look at these words.

> I don't know about tomorrow
> I just live from day to day
> I don't borrow from the sunshine
> For it's skies may turn to gray
> I don't worry o'er the future
> For I know what Jesus said
> And today He'll walk beside me
> For He knows what lies ahead
>
> Refrain:
> Many things about tomorrow
> I don't seem to understand
> But I know who holds tomorrow
> And I know who holds my hand
>
> Ev'ry step is getting brighter
> As the golden stairs I climb
> Ev'ry burden's getting lighter
> Ev'ry cloud is silver lined
> There the sun is always shining
> There no tear will dim the eye
> At the ending of the rainbow
> Where the mountains touch the sky
>
> Refrain:
> Many things about tomorrow
> I don't seem to understand
> But I know who holds tomorrow
> And I know who holds my hand

So my friends do not be threatened by this world or anything in it. Keep trusting God; He knows what's next and He will prepare us for it.

God bless you,
Fwfm; nlw

What Are You Preparing For?

What are your plans; what are you getting ready for? Whatever we are doing today it is preparing us for what is going to happen tomorrow. This is one reason we have to be careful what we get involved in.

Let's look at this from a good side. To become an NFL football player one should be playing Pop Warner football as a kid. Secondly they should play high school football.

This would lead to scholarships for college, then off to the pros. It's the same thing for basketball and baseball. Yes, there will be some hot days of practice and some possible rainy days, but it prepares you for future real games. Doctors just don't start operating, they have to go to college, take a MSAT (medical scholastic aptitude test). Then there is internship and residency. The more intense the job the more training is necessary. Training builds knowledge and character; be it professional or otherwise.

It just so happens God also trains the men who work for him. How does God do this, via various means? The men God used went via extensive training and many of them broke down during the training. For some reason God liked using the desert as training ground. God used the desert to train a lot of men like Abraham, Moses, Elijah, Paul, and etc.

There was something about the desert that clicked; this was beyond the Red Sea experiences and God's people being fed with manna and quail. God used the desert to prepare men to work the fight of spiritual warfare. Each time the men came out prepared and strong.

Part of preparation is having the right frame of mind. You have to want better to do better. When we are obedient to God he will take us to heights unknown to our imagination. "[20] Now unto him that is able to do exceeding abundantly above all that we ask or think, according to the power that worketh in us" (Eph. 3:20, KJV).

> [20–21] God can do anything, you know—far more than you could ever imagine or guess or request in your wildest dreams! He does it not by pushing us around but by working within us, his Spirit deeply and gently within us. (The Message)

God bless you,
Fwfm; nlw

How Great Is Hope?

Hope is the anchor of the soul. Hope gives one a healthy attitude; it brings comfort to the mind and heart, anticipating good things. The opposite is also true; a state of hopelessness and can drive one into depression. To believe what you're facing cannot be changed or resolved is a real downer.

When a person has lost all hope life looks like a long dark tunnel going nowhere. The Word even got in on it in Proverbs 13:12, "Hope deferred makes the heart sick."

Did you know a person without hope can become emotionally, physically, and even mentally ill? The lack of hope haunts them and makes them feel trapped in a bleak situation.

God would have you know that no situation is hopeless and there is a "b" portion to that same verse. "Desire fulfilled is a tree of life." The hope that anchors the believer's soul is none other than Christ. Knowing Jesus as Savior and Lord makes a difference. It affects our marriage, our family, our personal life, our job, our church, and everything else we're a part of.

We take all of our burdens and worries and concerns and cast them upon Christ and He assures us that He will not only handle them but never leave us or forsake us. Is that hope or what? When we cling to Him via whatever trials we're facing it brings hope.

He provides strength for our weary bodies, He gives peace to our anxious minds, and He brings comfort for our grieving hearts. That my friend is hope; basically He is the light at the end of the tunnel and He softly and tenderly leads and guides us via very desperate and trying situations. He anchors our souls in the midst of an unsteady and rocky world.

Do you realize Paul intentionally used the Word anchor in Hebrews 6:13–20)? An anchor was a popular image in the old Mediterranean world. The whole economy moved by shipping. The anchor symbolized safety, steadiness, and security. Half the old hymns mention "anchor." "I've anchored my soul in the Haven of Rest."

Paul wanted to remind us that God has given us a hope that holds firm in any storm. Oh, how great is that hope.

My hope is built on nothing less… We have a living hope; when we were born into it when we were born again. People without Christ have no foundation to base their expectations and desires so they live with a false sense of security to no security at all.

Nonbelievers make the assumption that what is important in this life is the material or physical, but we know via the Word (1 Tim. 6:9) that there is no safety in material things.

Those who pursue wealth and dreams discover many times too late that material things fail to satisfy. Believers anchor their hope in the solid rock of God. He is the same yesterday, today, and forever more. His name is Jesus. In times like these you need a Savior; In times like these you need and anchor…

You need someone whose words are always true and who always keeps His promises. Isn't it amazing how we sometimes project our unfulfilled desires upon God then argue that God left us wanting or He came up short?

No, if we submit to God's will we will always get an answer. It may not be what we want to hear, but it's an answer none the less— yes, no, or wait.

The Lord does not disappoint those who seek His will. We may feel temporarily let down when something we hope for is not in God's plan, but God never goes back on a biblical promise. You got what was best for you at the time for the purpose for which God had for you.

The best choice we can make in life is to choose Christ and Him crucified and make Him our hope. Whatever His will is for our life, seek that and turn from all else, it's only a distraction. Circumstances may shift and change, Jesus stays the same. He is a living hope who never disappoints.

God bless you,
Fwfm: nlw

How Do You Feel?

Isn't it amazing that many times no matter what we have or where we are, unhappiness finds its way into our life? Feelings just keep changing daily. Everything affects our feelings.

To help us in dealing with our feelings let us keep a few principles in mind.

1. We live in a hurry-up society or microwave world. Sort of a freeway life where we want everything at warp speed. We rush to work. We rush home. We rush through dealing with our kids and spouses. We don't realize it but all of this has a negative effect on our feelings. We really need to stop and smell the roses; there are always roses.

2. Do you really have to do "some things" or have you just told yourself that? What would really happen if you did not do those "things"? Put things in perspective and knock off the self-imposed pressures. No one is perfect even though it doesn't hurt to move in that direction. Ask God for daily plans.

3. Don't dwell on the past. Don't drive looking in the rearview mirror. Too much thought on negative; no wonder we are troubled. We should be concentrating on Phil. 4:8.

4. Try seeking God first in everything.

5. Check your attitude. Do you have an attitude because of your lot in life? How do you continually see things because it will certainly affect your feelings? Many times being

satisfied in God and all He has done changes our feelings completely. How you feel is associated with how you think. Go back to Phil. 4:8.

God bless you,
Fwfm; nlw

What's That about Peace?

Despite man's best efforts, the world's longing for peace remains unfulfilled. Every new generation has high hopes for everyone to get along but soon discover it's just not going to happen.

If you know the Word, peace can't happen until Christ return. Until then we as believers are called to be His ambassadors of peace. Just because we become a Christian it doesn't automatically change us into a people who pursue nothing but peace and harmony or kindness and unity. In us that is in our flesh dwelleth no good thing. We're born in sin and shaped in iniquity.

At times, we can be quick-tempered and impatient and it can be quite difficult to live in harmony with others. It's just so hard to let go of attitudes and habits that not only hurt ourselves but also others. You would think we would want to stop the madness, but we don't.

God has to transform us into Jesus's likeness. This can only happen after reading and applying the Word. The Holy Spirit will open our heart and minds causing us to think and act differently. We begin to say no to ungodliness thereby dispelling confusion and bring about peace in us and others.

All of our previous me-centered thinking is replaced with Christ-centered viewpoint. God patiently produces His fruit in us which includes love, joy, and peace (Gal. 5:22, 23).

So while the world keeps hoping for peace via man's solutions, we have figured out the only source of lasting peace comes via knowing and trusting Jesus as Savior and Lord of our lives.

Col. 3:15

Why do believers look and act different, it's the transforming power of Jesus and it affects everything we're involved in (our marriage, our families, our friendships, our jobs, and etc.).

God bless you,
Fwfm: nlw

We're Not Hopeless

Exodus 6:1–13

Sometimes it's kind of hard to believe or accept something new and different even when it's better and it excels us. Why, why is that, because we've been down for so long it's hard to believe we now have an opportunity to get up? It's not like we're saying we don't welcome the change, it's just that we have become so accustomed to being in the dumps.

Just like with these children of Israel, there can be a sense of hopeless resignation. I mean come on; they had been enslaved for over four hundred years now suddenly this Moses guy was going to free them because God said so? Well that all sounds good, in fact it sounds incredible. It's just hard to hear verse 9

They were so far down they couldn't look up. It's the same thing that happens to people in relationships. You meet a girl/guy and they treat you like dirt. You meet another one and they treat you even worse. Should a third one come along and treat you awful also you lose any self-esteem you had left. So finally you meet someone who thinks the world of you and can't understand why anyone would misuse you, but you can't believe you're getting this kind of respect.

Why is he/she respecting me, for so long no one else did? So you sabotage the relationship because you refuse to accept the respect because you believe you don't deserve it.

Is this what we're saying to God? Well God has something to say to us. The miraculous deliverance of His Covenant people (Hebrews) was an example of what He was going to do for us. This was a foreshadow of God's powerful intervention on our behalf via His Son Christ Jesus.

Just like God brought plagues on Egypt and opened up the Red Sea, He allowed Christ to be beaten and crucified for our salvation. I know, we said, "but Lord, I'm not worth anything, I'm just not worth your dying for me." But God said, 'While we were yet sinners Christ died for us…" The Word said, God so loved the world that He gave His only begotten Son… Wow, an adjective and a verb, He really loved us.

Here when we were powerless to help ourselves, Christ dies for us (sinful man) (Rom. 5:6). Let me tell you something, when life is at its lowest ebb, we are not without hope; why because of the wonderful grace of God. No one is hopeless whose hope is in God.

God bless you,
Fwfm: nlw

I Wish I Hadn't

Have you ever bought something and later wished you had not? Have you ever gone somewhere or been with someone and later wished you had not? Have you ever ate something and later wished you had not? Well that is what I want to talk about today.

Genesis 3:1–8 is where we are coming from. You can read it in the King James, Living Bible New International, or any text. It is about how the serpent spoke to Eve and convinced her that she should eat the apple from the forbidden tree.

I guess she didn't quite understand what God meant when he told her not to eat the fruit. But there is more that is missed upon reading the text. Eve was also told not to touch the fruit or she would die. So she should have thought in her mind, I can't touch this no matter what the circumstances or it's fatal.

God made it very clear to Adam and Eve; He put a keep away on that one tree and the tree was set aside in the midst of the garden. As an investigator I go to the different prisons daily. Some of the inmates wear certain colors and bracelets because they are to be kept away from others and it's quite clear by what they are wearing.

This is not to be ignored by the deputies as the consequences could be death to the inmate or other inmates. So back to Ms. Eve, why did she ignore God's clear warning? Now it gets rather confusing. A serpent spoke to her. First of all why was she listening to a serpent?

So just because this little slippery creature told her that God just didn't want her to be like him and that the fruit was really good to eat she ate, and not only so she gave her husband a piece also. So not only did she fall from grace, but she caused her husband to fall. This is what happens when we sin. We mess up and get the sticky poison on us, and then as if that is not bad enough, we pass the sticky poison on to someone else.

See right there, you have to be careful who you talk to and who you listen to. Immediately upon listening to this serpent Eve went and ate the fruit and gave a piece to Adam and their eyes were opened. They knew immediately something was not right. They did not die immediately but their eyes were opened to evil they had previously been protected from.

It was like a child being exposed to porn; their innocence was gone forever. Here they were walking around naked all this time and it was okay, but once they ate of the forbidden fruit they looked at themselves in shame and covered themselves.

Here is another interesting part. They were used to walking and talking with God daily in the Garden of Eden. When God came to speak with them on this day they ran and hid themselves among the trees. They also covered themselves with fig leaves.

Boy, what sin does to us; it makes us want to hide ourselves and what we have done. We know we are wrong, and we wonder if others know because the shame is all over our face. We start acting different because we are already convicted in our own mind. We have trespassed into an area we were forbidden and we know we should not have done this. We wish we hadn't. But it's too late now we did.

So now before we mess up, I beseech you in the name of Jesus, take His Word seriously. Do not stumble, mess up, whatever. Take God's Word seriously. If it says don't eat of this, don't eat. If it says can't touch this as it clearly did in Genesis 3:3b, then you can't touch it either.

Can I parenthetically say something? This might help many of us who are destined to mess up. Don't touch it, don't eat it, don't smell it, don't stare at it, dag nab it, stay away from it; it has a "keep away" on it. It's not good, no matter how it looks.

If you violate this rule it will no doubt have a bitter aftertaste no matter how it looked originally. You have trespassed; you have violated the rules. You have crossed the lines, you have blurred the lines and you shouldn't have. Now you must pay.

Adam and Eve's fall cost us all; they ate us out of house and home. They were kicked out of the Garden of Eden and did eventually die just as God said. They were exposed to evils that God originally protected them from until they ate of that forbidden fruit.

Even to think of things amiss is not good. James said be careful where you let your mind go because if you're not careful you'll find yourself doing the very things you think of. Clear your mind; clean your mind. IT didn't sneak up on you, you have been thinking of THIS all along and now you're doing it.

Now just like in Adam and Eve's case, God has to sacrifice blood. In their case He took an animal and slayed it to take its blood and skin and cover them. The Bible says the life of the flesh in is the blood...

In our case because sin as wracked us; and the wages of sin is death, Rom. 6:23: [23] For the wages of sin is death; but the gift of God is eternal life through Jesus Christ our Lord. He sent his Son, the Lord Jesus Christ to shed his blood so we might live...Wow! We violated him, but because He loved us so, he gave His life to re-establish us with His Father. Jesus acted as an extension cord or conduit. He reached one hand to God and the other to us. He extended himself; His blood. He washed us of our sin cleansing us to be acceptable to God once more. Wow!

As the scripture says in Romans 5:8, [8] But God commendeth his love toward us, in that, while we were yet sinners, Christ died for us.

Yeah, we wish we hadn't, but if you did go to 1 John 1:9, "[9] If we confess our sins, He is faithful and just to forgive us our sins and to cleanse us from all unrighteousness." Get the blood of Jesus, get right, and flee from sin.

God bless you,
Fwfm; nlw

Help me God, I Cannot Speak

We are not in this journey alone. God knew we would get weary and need help. Sometimes it is so bad we cannot find the right words and many times we cannot find any words at all. We search for God's will and we can't even find that. We have no idea what God is doing or why. We understand God allows things to happen and doesn't send mishap, but we feel we have had more than our share. We just can't get a handle on what we are dealing with; it's just too complex.

This is not uncommon; it has happened since biblical days. We are left confused, weary, and stressed. Does this remind you of King David? Does this remind you of Joseph? Look at Rom. 8:26, 27: "26 In the same way, the Spirit helps us in our weakness. We do not know what we ought to pray for, but the Spirit himself intercedes for us through wordless groans. 27 And he who searches our hearts knows the mind of the Spirit, because the Spirit intercedes for God's people in accordance with the will of God."

I know you already thought of Paul. He was beaten, stoned, jailed, abandoned and yet God tells him, 7 or because of these surpassingly great revelations. Therefore, in order to keep me from becoming conceited, I was given a thorn in my flesh, a messenger of Satan, to torment me. 8 Three times I pleaded with the Lord to take it away from me.

> 9 But he said to me, "My grace is sufficient for you, for my power is made perfect in weakness." Therefore I will boast all the more gladly about my weaknesses, so that Christ's power may rest on me. 10 That is why, for Christ's sake, I delight in weaknesses, in insults, in hardships, in perse-

cutions, in difficulties. For when I am weak, then I am strong. (2 Cor. 12:7–10)

The more Paul pleaded, the more desperate he became. No relief came; what did come was an understanding from God that he would endure despite the pain and discomfort with God to help. Wow!

Lastly, think about Jesus; God's own Son, his story is tremendous. Jesus own disciple and supposed friend betrayed him. Why, for 30 pieces of silver. All Jesus did was what was right and help people. All he did was heal the sick, give sight to the blind, and make the deaf hear. Heck he even raised the dead. For this he was lied on and beat to a pulp then crucified.

Yeah, this Christian thing is not easy to understand or accept. Jesus even asked God in Matthew 26:39, [39] Going a little farther, he fell with his face to the ground and prayed, "My Father, if it is possible, may this cup be taken from me. Yet not as I will, but as you will. "This was God's own Son crying out to Him from Gethsemane. Luke said, If they do this to the green tree, behold what will happen to the dry (23:31).

Jesus still had to go through with the salvation of man, and it hurt like hell. God knew what Jesus was facing and feeling and He knows what we are facing and feeling too. Jesus paid it all so we would not have too; that is how much He cared. He then left us the Holy Spirit.

The Holy Spirit was sent to comfort Christ and the Holy Spirit was also sent to comfort us. We can only understand so much as our perspective is finite. God's perspective is infinite and inclusive of all situations and circumstances we face.

God sends the Holy Spirit to comfort, touch, lead, and guide us. He will lift our burdens and give us clarity if we allow him to. Even when we cannot speak because our load is too heavy, the Holy Spirit will hear our groan and take that to God.

The Holy Spirit will fill in the words when we cannot speak. The Holy Spirit dwells within us and knows our mind and heart. He speaks to our spirit opening us up to the will of God and His Word.

The very fact that God gives His spirit to all believers proves the value He places on preparing us for this world of cosmos. We must communicate with Him as He is our Father. When we lose sight or lose the words to speak, the Holy Spirit will assist us. What better helper is there to pep and cheer us in becoming responsible, wise, and strong children of God?

Yes, there will be times we simply are doing so bad we cannot speak, but our helper will interpret and send that prayer to God. God's will is made clearer to us via the Holy Spirit now we must submit and yield our will to His.

God bless you,
Fwfm; nlw

The Paradox of Sanctification

> ¹² And so, my dear friends, just as you have always obeyed,
> not only when I was with you but even more now that I
> am absent, continue to work out your salvation with fear
> and trembling.¹³ For it is God who is producing in you
> both the desire and the ability to do what pleases him.
> — Phil. 2:12, 13

The Christian life calls for positive moral action and obedience on our part. It also calls for confident expectation that God will do all he has promised. We must not do the old "Let go and let God," we must submit and help God take us where He wants us to be.

Here is the paradox, Paul asserts that we have died and yet we live. He claimed to be sorrowful yet always rejoicing. Having nothing yet possessing all things. He was poor yet made rich. How about work out your salvation for it is God who works in you.

Please keep in mind there are two aspects of holy living—what God does, and what we must do. We don't wait for God to perform the miracle of deliverance and sanctification; we give Him our active cooperation.

Human with the divine it is fatal to ignore or play down either aspect. Yes, sometimes it can be difficult trying to determine where God's part ends and man's begins but it is the ministry of the Holy Spirit to illuminate the difference showing us the truth. It is up to us to then honestly know and seek that truth.

Faith is a vital element in sanctification but it is not attained apart from man's cooperation. Paul helps us with these scriptures. "22 That ye put off concerning the former conversation the old man, which is corrupt according to the deceitful lusts" (Eph. 4:22).

> "[24]And those who are Christ's have crucified the flesh with its passions and desires" (Gal 5:24).
> "[13] For if you live according to the flesh you will die; but if by the Spirit you put to death the deeds of the body, you will live" (Rom. 8:13).

Now this may sound complex, but it is actually quite simple. You cannot continue to do what you did or were doing and expect change, cleanliness, or sanctification. You will remain dirty because you are still kicking dirt up on you. You must change your ways and you change you. The Holy Spirit will do the rest, but you must submit to Him.

The paradox is you have been given an estate, now go to work and develop its hidden resources. You have been saved from the guilt, power, and penalty of sin but you have NOT been saved from sin.

You will occasionally mess up until the day of Christ, but you should be at least leaning toward righteousness. It is a life job. The race is not given to the swift or to the strong but to he who endures to the end. God does not exhort us to action without providing adequate motive and incentive to encourage us to attain the highest in life and character.

We are not left on our own. [23] Jesus answered and said to him, "if anyone loves Me, he will keep My word; and My Father will love him, and We will come to him and make Our home with him" (John 14:23).

God will never leave us or forsake us Heb. 13:5, 6: He will stay with us all the way through our life. In Phil. 1:6, being confident of this very thing, that He who hath begun a good work in you will perform it until the Day of Jesus Christ Not only does God dwell in the believer's heart, but He is at work there as the active agent in our sanctification.

Another paradox; how impossible it would be for man to force tons of water through solid wood. Yet God does it every day via nature a thousand times as sap rises via trees.

In sanctification God and man are joined at the hip. They are inextricably tied together. Any effort to separate the two ruins everything. Man's will is submitted to God's will to give it action and power and leadership. Without God's will man goes off on a tangent.

Without God to sanctify us we become like Paul said in Romans 7:18: "[18] For I know that in me (that is, in my flesh,) dwelleth no good thing: for to will is present with me; but how to perform that which is good I find not."

I have the desire to do good but I cannot carry it out. I see a better course and I approve but I follow the worse course. We simply lack the disposition to do the better thing even though we know it is right. We are paralyzed without Christ Holy Spirit working in us. We need the power of God to resolve, perform, and execute His perfect will.

To rely on our resources is to beckon failure. It is our choice. Once the right impulse has been supplied by God giving us the power to resolve whatever issue is before us it still remains in us to act.

Sanctification pushes us to act, not iust not doing wrong things but to also do the right thing, good things. So sanctification reminds us that in and of ourselves we have no power. However the divine indwelling power of God via the Holy Spirit works in us. We are no longer the play toy of weakness and sin. We have been sanctified.

God bless you,
Fwfm; nlw

Lord, Must It Be This Way?

Sometimes it's hard to believe God is aware of our anguish, because if He only knew about this He would do thus and thus. Well. He knows, He's omniscient, He's also sovereign; nothing gets by God. Whatever you're going through, it has to be this way, but don't lose hope. Keep trusting God and submit your every care to Him. It is an acknowledgement to Him that you know He is aware and you trust Him for the outcome.

Sometimes up and sometimes down, sometimes almost level to the ground. Through sick and via sin, via thick and via thin, God will see you through. It will not always be pretty, ask Job, check chapter 1 and 2. God says very clearly in His Word that "His ways are not like our ways" (Isa.55:8). God has a way of involving Himself in every area of our lives as we open the door (Rev. 3:20) to conform us into the image of Christ (Rom 8:28, 29).

Let's just be clear about something; Jesus life was no cakewalk, it wasn't even semisweet. He suffered, and He bled for us. He was wounded for our transgressions, bruised for our iniquities, and the chastisement of our peace was laid upon Him… (Isa. 53:1–6).

If they did it to the green tree behold what shall they do to the dry (Luke 23:31).

Each of us is surrounded by God's protection and care, but we will go via our vicissitudes of life. God will always do right by us, but that doesn't mean keeping us from having troubles all the time. This is how it is in the cosmos; it must be this way. Thank God for the by and by when the morning comes and we no longer have to put up with the way of this world.

God bless you,
Fwfm: nlw

When Peace Like a River

Peace is essential, necessary and important; we must have it. Peace affects us intellectually, emotionally and physically. We can be robbed of a lot of things but if we still have peace within we will be all right. Uncertainty about tomorrow can rob us only if we allow it to.

When we really know Jesus we don't have to be desperate, feel threatened or panic. Our God has promised us that no matter what is going on around us in the world we must not let it ravage our mind, our soul or our heart.

Look at these scriptures of how God wanted to reassure us.

> [8] We are troubled on every side, yet not distressed; we are perplexed, but not in despair;
> [9] Persecuted, but not forsaken; cast down, but not destroyed;
> [10] Always bearing about in the body the dying of the Lord Jesus, that the life also of Jesus might be made manifest in our body. (2 Cor. 4:8–10)

> [5] Let your conversation be without covetousness; and be content with such things as ye have: for he hath said, I will never leave thee, nor forsake thee. [6] So that we may boldly say, The Lord is my helper, and I will not fear what man shall do unto me. (Heb. 13:5, 6)

> [31] What shall we then say to these things? If God be for us, who can be against us?

[32] He that spared not his own Son, but delivered him up for us all, how shall he not with him also freely give us all things?

[33] Who shall lay any thing to the charge of God's elect? It is God that justifieth.

[34] Who is he that condemneth? It is Christ that died, yea rather, that is risen again, who is even at the right hand of God, who also maketh intercession for us.

[35] Who shall separate us from the love of Christ? shall tribulation, or distress, or persecution, or famine, or nakedness, or peril, or sword?

[36] As it is written, For thy sake we are killed all the day long; we are accounted as sheep for the slaughter.

[37] Nay, in all these things we are more than conquerors through him that loved us.

[38] For I am persuaded, that neither death, nor life, nor angels, nor principalities, nor powers, nor things present, nor things to come,

[39] Nor height, nor depth, nor any other creature, shall be able to separate us from the love of God, which is in Christ Jesus our Lord. (Rom. 8:31–39, KJV)

Now look at the same text in The Message.

[31-39] So, what do you think? With God on our side like this, how can we lose? If God didn't hesitate to put everything on the line for us, embracing our condition and exposing himself to the worst by sending his own Son, is there anything else he wouldn't gladly and freely do for us? And who would dare tangle with God by messing with one of God's chosen? Who would dare even to point a finger? The One who died for us—who was

raised to life for us!—is in the presence of God at this very moment sticking up for us. Do you think anyone is going to be able to drive a wedge between us and Christ's love for us? There is no way! Not trouble, not hard times, not hatred, not hunger, not homelessness, not bullying threats, not backstabbing, not even the worst sins listed in Scripture:

[2] When thou passest through the waters, I will be with thee; and through the rivers, they shall not overflow thee: when thou walkest through the fire, thou shalt not be burned; neither shall the flame kindle upon thee. (Isa. 43:2)

Do you really still think you're alone or God doesn't have your back? The peace of God brings about wholeness, a whole new quality of life even in the midst of conflict. God says over and over again in his Word, fear not. Why does God keep telling us not to fear, because fear destroys our peace? Fear debilitates us.

People who are constantly afraid hurt themselves and others. One writer said broken hurt people hurt people; this is so true. We all need some form of peace in our life or we are no good to ourselves or others. This is why many people are awful partners in relationships, they have no inner peace.

[1]Let not your heart be troubled: ye believe in God, believe also in me. But wait that is not all; not only am I going to take care of you now, also in the future. Look at the next verses;
[2] In my Father's house are many mansions: if it were not so, I would have told you. I go to prepare a place for you.
[3] And if I go and prepare a place for you, I will come again, and receive you unto myself; that where I am, there ye may be also.

[4] And whither I go ye know, and the way ye know.
(John 14:1–4)

In case you didn't know it, the heart pumps our life blood; we can't live without a heart. The heart is also our spiritual seat of understanding. We must not allow our heart to become contaminated or destroyed by lack of peace. When we know and have a good relationship with Christ it keeps our heart from being stirred or disturbed. Fear and confusion must not reign, not when we serve a living God via Christ our Lord.

Jesus has given us something to believe in something good. That is why the songwriter wrote this song and you ought to Google it for the melody.

> Something beautiful, something good
> All my confusion He understood
> All I had to offer Him was brokenness and strife
> But he made something beautiful of my life.

What a resume, what safety, don't you just love him; our savior? This is a serious lifeboat of peace. You can trust him no matter what you are going through or what you are facing. He says here is my record, here is my CV.

From birth to resurrection we know with whom our trust is in. This is not even counting every victory in the Word or in our lives.

Jesus is not giving us empty words but actual actions which ought to remove our heartache and give us peace. The Word says [4] You are of God, little children, and have overcome them, because He who is in you is greater than he who is in the world. (1 Jn. 4:4).

We ought to seek and feel secure in his presence. What you see in this life is not all there is; there is so much more to come.

God bless you,
Fwfm; nlw

In the Night Hour

Does the night time scare you? Does it make you uneasy because you cannot see? Yes, a lot of bad things happen in the night hour. Another way of looking at it is did you know that God is the one who created the night hour for our sleep and restoration?

Now just because we are sleep and unaware of what goes on or have no control of anything while we rest, it doesn't mean it is the same for God. Look at Psalms 121:2–4.

> 2 My help cometh from the Lord, which made heaven and earth.
> 3 He will not suffer thy foot to be moved: he that keepeth thee will not slumber.
> 4 Behold, he that keepeth Israel shall neither slumber nor sleep.

God's works doesn't cease just because we closed our eyes. Our human eyes limit us in seeing in the dark. Our humanness (finite) also keeps us from seeing things in the spiritual realm. However God is infinite and can see in the dark and all spiritual mysteries. We cannot and we must not put human limitations on God.

God can and will intervene as He sees fit. Sometimes that means deliverance, or it may mean protection. The Lord who keeps us neither slumbers nor sleeps. It was in the night when the Medes and the Persians took over Babylon (Dan. 5:1–31). It was in the night when the first born of Egypt was smote unless they had Passover blood of the lamb on their doorpost (Exodus 12:1–36).

It was in the night when Nicodemus came to Jesus and was told he must be born again (John 3:1–21). It was in the night when Judas betrayed Jesus (John 13:21–30). It was in the late night and early morning when Jesus got up from the tomb he had been buried in for three days (Matt. 28:1, 2).

While the world slept God had raised His Son to life. So as we can see all throughout history God has accomplished miraculous things under the cover of darkness or night In the night hour; night time may be a negative thing for us but for God it is altogether different.

God bless you,
Fwfm; nlw

Waiting

Part I

Just like going via the seasons waiting can be tough. Winters can be harsh. Oh, if spring would just get here already. Some of us have been waiting for a husband or waiting for a wife. Some of us have been waiting for better health, a job, finances, or a child. Some of us have been waiting while we try to overcome some compulsive sin and etc. All this time and we're still dealing with the same thing and we don't even see any buds of growth or fruit.

As much as we may not want to, this is a good time to ascertain just what kind of seeds we have we been sowing or planting. The reason I say this is because many times in our season of waiting we become impatient and say or do some things that may very well be contrary to God's will. If in fact that is the case and we've sown seeds of discord, ingratitude, or sin, are we then prepared to reap a harvest of weeds and thorns?

Many times the reason we keep getting a bum crop or no crop is in direct proportion to what we are planting. In other cases that is simply our lot; we must wait on God and let Him work His time schedule. You cannot make yourself have a child; that is a gift from God. You can do all the preparation, but God still has to give the gift of life. You will yield fruit in your season as per Psalms 1:3. (Google.)

I know with this particular example it can be grueling and painful like with Hannah. You just have to keep humbly praying and leaving it in God's hands. Don't let your attitude or personality become sour or cross because God has not granted your desire. In a situation like this don't over analyze it either, just keep praying, God hears you; it's not in vain.

I know unemployment is high, marriages and families are at an all-time low and suffering. I know many people are looking for a good spouse. Again, this is more fixable than having a child, but you must trust God and wait. You don't want to jump the gun or jump the broom. Better to be in the right place with the right person than in a hell hole which constantly eats at you like a cancer.

Waiting on God is not easy. Satan offers you cheap substitutes to pacify you and unfortunately many of us accept them. Just like in Farming 101, you have to till the ground, plant the right seed and wait. There are a lot of factors or variables here that you have no control over like the weather and such. You must wait on God; He will bless the soil, send the right weather, and keep the bugs away without killing the fruit.

We get caught up in; if it doesn't happen by this date I'm going to do such and such. Are you giving God an ultimatum? God knows your need and he will never forsake you, but you do have to trust Him and wait. Isaiah 55:8, 9 says, "8 For my thoughts are not your thoughts, neither are your ways my ways," declares the Lord. 9 "As the heavens are higher than the earth, so are my ways higher than your ways and my thoughts than your thoughts.

Stop trying to figure it out or explain it: it is what it is.

Ask God for what you need then say, "Lord, please grant it if it is your will. I know you know best despite my desire so Lord not my will but thine be done." Now mean this and wait on God as you ask daily, still thank Him and praise Him for who He is and what He has already done. Some time in our waiting it is so painful and it has been so long until all we can do is groan. Our very soul aches as we have been waiting for our request for so long. We literally feel forgotten about (Rom. 8:26).

In the same way, the Spirit helps us in our weakness. We do not know what we ought to pray for, but the Spirit himself intercedes for us with groans that words cannot express.

Let me tell you this, if it's worth having, it's worth waiting for. The deeper your soul longs and groans while you continue to humbly petition God, the sweeter the gift when it arrives. Healthy relationships, good jobs, wonderful children, don't just happen; they take time and lots of prayer and preparation.

God hears our cry and pities our every groan. In His time He will bless us accordingly. Please do not lose heart while you wait. Please do not accept wooden nickels or cheap substitutes. Wait on God and let Him show you a better way however long it takes. With God holding your hand at least you have assurance.

God bless you,
Fwfm: nlw

Did I Ever Tell You about the Time?

How do you know when you belong to a certain group or family/ you listen to the history of that group or family and you identify. This is why grandpa or grandma told those old stories over and over again.

Throughout the OT God commanded the Israelites to tell stories to their children—stories about where God brought them from and how faithful He had been to them over the years. Stories of his grace and mercy and deliverance; God wanted every generation to know what He had done for them. Why? These reasons:

1. Never forget where you came from and what you came through.
2. So the people could understand that they were set apart from the pagan nations around them. They were a chosen people.

The parents and elders were to tell the story over and over again, Passover, how God brought them via the desert, fed them, Red Sea experiences, and etc.

Before they get to the Promised Land make sure they remember it was I, Yahweh, Jehovah…, who brought them.

What's the point of giving you more and better if you don't even appreciate what you already have? Lord, if I had this amount of money I would do such and such… You're not even responsible with the little you have now, why should I bless you with more?

After God parted the flooded Jordan River (just like He parted the Red Sea), the Lord commanded a representative from each of the twelve tribes to take a stone from the riverbed and build an altar on the shore.

Later on when their children would ask what the monument meant they were to say, "Did I ever tell you about the time…" (Josh. 4:6, 7).

Do you remember your difficult years? Do you remember how God brought you through? Do you remember His comfort and His peace? How did those bills get paid? How did you make it via that divorce? How did you make it when you lost your job? How did you make it when your friends turned their backs on you?

If it had not been for the Lord on my side, tell me where would I be…?

God brought me via the difficult times and every now and then I've got to tell somebody… Did I ever tell you…?

Its stories like this that underscore God's love and faithfulness to us. It helps your children remember were it not for the Lord, where would we be?

Who brought you via your miscarriages? Who brought you via your sickness? When you thought all was lost because you lost a loved one, who held your hand and reassured you?

It was God. Oh great is Thy faithfulness…

These stories bond a family. (Teachable moments.) These stories let friends understand this is who I am; this is where I've come from. These stories teach strangers/co-workers, this is the reason I live like I live, sing like I sing…

Deuteronomy 6:7

So the next time you're driving down the road and one of your parents starts up and say, "Did I ever tell you…" let 'em finish without crossing your eyes or taking a deep breath. There's a method to their madness.

Oh, victory in Jesus, my Savior forever…

It's so when you meet life…you can be prepared. When life grabs you by the ankles and turns you upside down you can say, "Give me that old time religion…"

God bless you,
Fwfm: nlw

Maybe Your Box Is Too Small

Ephesians 2:5–8
Romans 5:20

It's so easy to be judgmental in life; we put people in brackets, boxes categories, when we actually should have relationships. Christ didn't categorize us; He had a relationship with us. Categories are easy; relationships are messy.

It's quite easy not to feel for someone or extend grace as long as you think in terms of categories. It's easy to be judgmental when you don't know any names, or even real faces. Then once you discover the real truth or hear the full story suddenly you go, "Now I understand."

When Jesus deals with us we find full grace and full truth. He doesn't give us half and half. He fully forgives—He doesn't say to the woman caught in adultery, "You made a mistake" or "Be careful." He says, "Go and sin no more."

This is what the church is called to do, let it go, move on, but be firm in reaching out with love. It may be stern but it's fair. Any of us could and will fall; do we just forget about it, no; we call them on it, then we forgive them and move on (Gal. 6:1).

If we are Bible readers and church goers our faith and understanding of grace ought to evolve. Being in a marriage, being a parent and etc. all of these relationships evolve. We grow via experience and understanding. Those of us who resist this growth or transformation we are robbing ourselves and others of real grace and forgiveness.

Our old mind tells us "we just can't let people off." You're not letting people off you're showing grace because it's the proper thing to do. Do you think refusing to forgive someone teaches them anything? Half of the time people we refuse to forgive don't even know it. They certainly don't feel punished, it's like administering a whipping or a poison and taking it yourself.

Grace is extended to anyone without feeling they are being let off, because Christ extended it to us. Paul wrote in Romans 2:4, "the kindness of God leads to repentance." If Christianity is primarily about a relationship with God then refusal to forgive and demanding retribution should take a back seat to love and grace.

This is what Jesus did and this is what we should do. People who knew nothing about Jesus liked Him because He sought to help and extend grace.

Listen, let's get something clear, you can accept people without approving of something they do. We should (like Jesus) communicate complete acceptance without communicating approval.

E. G. look at parents saying, "I absolutely love you, but I don't approve of what you did." So a child can't say, "Well, you don't love me or you don't accept me, because the parent can then say, "this is not an acceptance issue; this is an approval issue. So if we can keep these two categories clear then we can cross over toward a new type relationship without fear of being judged.

Nevertheless the truth is we have closed ourselves off to people who seemingly don't accept us. So if our concern is behavior or judging we must alter that. We must show acceptance of them as a person, not approval of their behavior. We don't want them to get the impression that we condone what they do; but they will at least have some relationship with us because they know we accept them. This then leads to some influence.

Many a relationship has been lost because the other party felt they were never accepted. (Marriage, children, etc.) Jesus was able to say to that woman caught in adultery, "I don't approve of what you did, but I accept you."

Acceptance paves the way to influence. So for some church member (alleged Christian) to say, "because I don't approve, I won't accept," maybe your box is too small.

You ought to think outside your box because you just missed a perfect opportunity to influence. Harmless as a dove and cunning as a fox…He that winneth souls must be wise.

This is why "born again" is the model—not "behaved again." Sure you can stay in your box and judge…or you can extend grace and get outside your box realizing that your box was too small to begin with.

Think of it like this, instead of categories, think relationships. Father/child, parent/child; there are tensions in being a mother/father; you have to also be a parent.

If God really is "Father" then I can be a wayward son but still a son. I can be a prodigal son, but still a son. The relationship is there even though there are some approval issues that need to be resolved.

Grace allows what has been a real tough relationship to be one that can be healed-but it will take forgiveness. It's so powerful if one of you would just go first it draws the other in. Doesn't it remind you of "while we were yet sinners Christ died for the ungodly…"?

Jesus went first, that's what grace does. Grace says I'm not going to wait; I'm not going to meet you in the middle, I'm going first… oh, how powerful.

How many of you have been told or showed, "your kindness has led me to repentance?" We live under the canopy of forgiveness and grace. So it should be like a great marriage. With a parent/child, I don't obey because I'm scared, I obey because I know she loves and accepts me, she just didn't like what I did. I know she has my best interest at heart.

In the Garden of Eden, God's relationship with man was broken over an issue of trust, so it makes sense that it would be restored over an issue of trust. Anything less becomes obligation—that creates tension and it's not the end game or God's goal.

The overflow of my gratitude to God should be the extension of grace to others. We owe—we owe everything to God. Yet we could not pay because the price was too high, too expensive. What did God do, He extended us grace, and we should do the same to others. Jesus paid it all…

God bless you,
Fwfm; nlw

You Have to Cleanse the Temple

¹² Then Jesus went into the Temple and threw out everyone
who was selling and buying in the Temple, and overturned the
moneychanger's tables and the chairs of those who sold doves. ¹³ He
told them, "It is written, 'My house is to be called a house of prayer,
but you are turning it into a hideout for bandits! (Den of thieves).
—Matthew 21:12, 13

You certainly remember this story of how Jesus went into the temple and whipped the money changers out. The church was supposed to be for helping people not for making profit or money. The temple was contaminated back then with dishonest people and it is also contaminated now. Minister or not, many church folk will do almost anything for a few coins (ask Judas).

So sometimes you have to cleanse the temple. The church of God is supposed to be a house of prayer not a den of thieves and perverts. Luke 19:46 saying to them, "It is written, 'My house shall be a house of prayer, but you have made it a den of robbers.'"

People come for cleansing, comfort, and peace and leave confused broke and broken. Women and children sexually abused and all in the name of the clergy collar or church. Yes, sometimes you have to cleanse the temple.

God expects more from those who know better. Those who know better must do better. Not only does this apply to the church but also to our living temple; our bodies. We cannot put just anything in our bodies (alcohol, drugs, illicit sex, and etc.) yet expect our bodies to hold up under this type weight.

[19] You know that your body is a sanctuary of the Holy Spirit, who is in you, a temple whom you have received from God, don't you? You do not belong to yourselves. (1 Cor. 6:19)

I know you don't hear it often or perhaps at all now because it's not popular but I beseech you brethren by the mercies of God; cleanse your temple or suffer the consequences.

How can we possibly be healed when we are constantly defiling the very place that is supposed to be clean (our temple)? That would be like pouring mud in the washing machine. I beckon your attention to this matter; please cleanse your temple. It will make a major difference in your spiritual healing and life.

God bless you,
Fwfm; nlw

Yes, God Loves You Despite the Circumstances

Wow, has the world changed. Oh how quickly our lives can be altered. We've lost jobs, relationships, loved ones, and the storm is still brewing. It's only natural that people are looking for an outlet or something to plug the dike; I mean we have literally been bombarded. Unfortunately, many people have found the wrong shelter. It may bring comfort temporarily, but over all its worse than the storm; i.e. alcohol, immoral or illicit activity, drugs-prescription or otherwise, and etc. These are not remedies; at best they are "distractions."

If you're going to seek refuge, be careful to go to the right place. Sometimes it's better to be left in an alleged low place than to be picked up by just anyone or anything (Rom. 8:28, 31–32, 35, 37–39).

No matter what you face in life believe the Word of God can and will make an awesome difference and give you victory. Now let me just give you a few simple truths to assist you. First of all, "Yes, God loves you despite the circumstances." God is still in control despite what it looks like. You will overcome every obstacle blocking your path in which God is directing you. Yes, there will be trials, and yes God will allow many of them, but they are there to make you better not bitter or sour you on life. God has your best interest at heart (Mt. 7:9–11). God will provide a way out of no way (Ps. 37:25). God takes full responsibility for your care. Who is more responsible than God?

He will always be with you even to the end (Heb. 13:5, 6; John 14:18; Ps. 23:4). I know; others who made promises have left you and abandoned you; well we're talking about God here. You may leave Him but He will never forsake you. You are sealed with His Holy Spirit (Eph. 4:30). You will always have a powerful friend, counselor, and advocate with you to heal, to help, to comfort, and etc. "Yes, God loves you despite the circumstances" (Rom. 5:8, 1 John 4:7–10).

God's affection for you is not based on what you do or what you go through, but on His grace. You can rejoice, God is still in control.

God bless you,
Fwfm; nlw

Emotional Baggage

²² Cast your burden on the Lord, And He shall sustain you;
   He shall never permit the righteous to be moved.
                                                    —Psalm 55:22

⁷ Casting all your care upon Him, for He cares for you.
                                                    —1 Peter 5:7

Emotional baggage is a term used to refer to the feelings, thoughts, patterns and past experiences that continue to traumatize a person each time they are triggered or recalled. They also affect a person's behavior and responses to life.

Emotional baggage keeps a person in spiritual bondage. They can't be the kind of person God wants them to be. All the freedom that Jesus offers and longs to give are ultimately kept from this individual because they refuse to deal with the baggage.

These bags are heavy burdens and we need to be released from their crushing weight. We should go back and read the aforementioned scriptures over and over again and make them a part of our lives.

Some people feel guilty at lying down their past. They feel as if that also removes the validity of the past relationships or whatever. It is really all about forgiving, forgetting, and releasing. We must learn to give it to Jesus, let him free you; that stuff is not in your circle of influence.

There is nothing as comforting, encouraging, uplifting, or joyful as casting off the weight of emotional baggage and walking away freely in life.

Try this prayer for starting your year off right. Father why do I hang on to things that hinder me from experiencing your fullness and the fullness of abundant life? Help me unload this baggage and lighten my load.

I want to lay down my burdens by the riverside and study war no more; help me Lord. In Jesus's name, amen.

God bless you,
Fwfm; nlw

It is God, Not Elijah

2 Kings 2:13–18

Elisha picks up the cloak or mantle that had fallen from Elijah; he then went back and stood on the bank of the Jordan. He raised the old cloak (the symbol of Elijah's prophetic office to which he succeeded). He raised it over head in imitation of Elijah's act and brought it down on the waters…and nothing happened.

So he did it again…v. 14 saying, Lord, where are you, where is the God of Elijah? Well, first let's get something clear; it was never Elijah doing these great works, it was always God. So the mantle was symbolic at best, like communion…

Question: Was this despair or query in the question. E. G. (Mt. Moriah lost their pastor). What happens when you lose a loved one who had great influence? Do you cover the pastor's chair with a white sheet so no one can sit there again? No, you get another pastor.

No one is essential but God.

I'll tell you what happens, you must go on. They would want you to go on; not only so God still remains, and He will help you to go on.

Joshua was told, be strong and of good courage for God is with you three times in the first nine verses of chapter one. The point is, don't worry about Moses Joshua, he's gone. Don't worry about Elijah Elisha, he's gone. They didn't have power; they had God; now you have God too.

It wasn't Elijah doing the miracles, it was God. There's no power in his mantle, his manner, or his methods. Elijah's power was that of the Living God.

So Elisha by faith and with newly restored confidence struck the water again and it departed, and he crossed over.

Now, a whole lot of young prophets or seminary students (fifty) were watching this whole thing. They didn't see the chariots of fire, but they saw that Elijah was missing. So they ran to Elisha, bowed down and greeted him with respect. They knew from having just witnessed the parting of the waters that the same Spirit of God that rested on Elijah was now filling Elisha.

Now here is where you begin to see that they couldn't see like Elisha. They said, God bless you, sir (v. 16a).

No, don't worry about it, the Lord took him. They still couldn't see. It doesn't matter how many times you say it or how you Say it, if they can't see, or if they don't have the same faith relationship, you're not going to get them to see.

Try explaining to the Catholics that there is something wrong with bowing down to saints no matter how holy you believed them to be.

Try explaining to Catholics, okay this pedophile activity, enough already; there has been too much cover-up and not enough discipline by the church. They can't see...

v. 17 They insisted, they persisted, but we must go, we're sure the Spirit of the Lord has carried Elijah to a mountain or valley. No, no, yes, yes.

They kept asking until Elisha felt ashamed like they thought he just didn't care. Okay, go ahead.

Three days they searched, nothing. Listen, it doesn't matter how diligent your search; if your premise is off-based, all is in vain. They came back exhausted, worn out, discouraged, we don't understand... No, you don't, and no you wouldn't because you can't see. God gave the pastor a vision; He told him where he wants to take the church. It's up to pastor who to be obedient and make it happen. Of course there will be some folk along the way who say, well I just don't see it; no you wouldn't, because the vision was given to the pastor. The accountability and responsibility lies with him.

Elisha said I told you not to go. He waited for them v. 18 and when they returned empty handed he told them, follow me as I follow God. So often God raises us an individual to do a unique work in a special way and empowers him/her by His Spirit to do that work. Someone else comes along and attempts to duplicate that work thinking that person had power. We later find out, it wasn't Elijah, but it was God.

Give honor to whom you will, but don't dishonor God in the process...

A good mother/father, husband/wife, leader is wonderful, but they are not God. If you're going to imitate, imitate faith (Heb. 13:7, 9).

Don't be like the Philistines who stole the Ark of the Covenant thinking it had magical powers in it; they later found out it was God...

It's not about Elijah, it's about God...

God bless you,
Fwfm: nlw

Where Is Your Focus?

We are told so much nowadays until we literally don't know what or who to believe. What we should know is we can and should always trust the Bible. The Word admonishes us to keep up with our life.

What is going on, are we growing, are we using our time wisely? I work as a private investigator a lot so I get paid by how much time is used. At times I am so busy until what matters more is not how long I am at a location, but moving on to other people and places to investigate.

When I lose that time because I am in the jail too long, or in the courts too long, I can't get that time back. Now I still have to talk to witnesses and write reports and I am out of time because I spend too much time at the jail or court so I miss an interview. My point is, how we spend our time is important because we can't get that back, it's irrevocable.

So because time is such a precious commodity it is foolish to waste it. If business time is as important as I have just explained, spiritual time is even more important. We cannot and we must not keep wasting time while our spiritual life fleets in front of us. Where is our focus; what is important to us? Where are our priorities? Does our marriage and family matter? If so what are we doing to improve and keep them? Does our health matter; how is our diet and exercise?

Does knowing God matter if so what are we doing to keep the faith? We already know it is obviously going to be constantly challenged? If we are not reading the Word, fellowshipping with the right people, listening to the right Word and praying, we are wasting valuable time. Our values or spiritual matters will diminish because that is not our focus or priority.

To keep putting off God or putting off prayer and Bible study until later is dangerous and foolish. When we get attacked we want to be prepared already. The old saying is "I would rather prepare for a storm that never comes then not prepare and the storm does come."

That is because you won't have time in the storm, it is upon you, you've already squandered the preparation time. Now it is rush, rush, rush and that is rarely good for anyone. Whatever you value will get your focus. Think about it and get your focus in the proper perspective.

God bless you,
Fwfm; nlw

The Value of Stress

A family was out shopping one day and went into a potter's shack. The place was cramped as it was too small for all the people playing looky-loo. Eventually most of the crowd left, but one family decided to stay because their kids seemed interested in the pottery.

They noticed two shelves of finished vases, one on either side of the potter. With childlike innocence one of the kids reached out to touch a vase. The potter said, "Please don't touch the pottery on that shelf, you'll ruin it." Then in surprise to everyone he said, "Why don't you touch the ones on the other shelf?"

Of course everyone was curious why some vases could be touched but not others. Pointing to the "do not touch" shelf the potter explained, "These haven't been via the fire yet." You see there is more to making pottery than just making beautiful shapes and masterpieces out of blobs of clay. Once they are formed they have to bake at a certain temperature to make sure they hold their shape. If they get touched before the fire they are quickly marred and dented. Without the fire the vase is pretty, but it's fragile.

The other vases could be touched because they had twice been baked in his kiln at temperatures exceeding two thousand degrees. The heat makes the clay firm and strong. The fire makes the beauty last without being pushed out of shape.

(1 Pet. 1:6, 7, NIV), [6] In all this you greatly rejoice, though now for a little while you may have had to suffer grief in all kinds of trials. [7] These have come so that the proven genuineness of your faith—of greater worth than gold, which perishes even though refined by fire— may result in praise, glory and honor when Jesus Christ is revealed.

Both Peter and this potter were talking to me about a fire that increases the value of something precious. There is a heat that burns, and another heat that beautifies. There is a God-produced, Father-filtered stress and then there is the world's stress. Overworked, too much on your schedule, not enough rest/recreation, no Bible reading or study, little prayer equals little power… You can't just keep spinning your wheel you wear out. You have to stop and take account.

God is trying to get us to seek peace through Him. He wants us to manage our stress via Him. The heat He brings will prove, strengthen, and beautify. Personal peace is not the elimination of stress it is the management of stress. If we live without pressure we become fragile as a potter's unfired vase.

God has skillfully reshaped us on His wheel, making a "big blob" into something beautiful, something valuable. The songwriter said, "Something beautiful, something good, all my confusion, He understood, all I had to offer him was brokenness and strife but he made something beautiful of my life. What others had thrown away and considered refuse, God redeemed it and said, "You're beautiful."

We need to eliminate self-induced stress and allow the pressure of God to shape us and form us. If the pressure is taken off a piece of coal, there will be no diamond. Removing that irritating grain of sand from an oyster's tummy means having no pearl. Don't help a caterpillar in his struggle inside his cocoon; it is going via metamorphosis, if you remove the pressure/struggle you will doom him it to be a worm for the rest of its life.

The proper amount and proper kind of pressure or irritation and pain can be tools to develop. God may send a load, but He will never send an overload. The right pressure doesn't make you bitter it makes you better. The apple and peach tree and rose bush have to be cut by the pruning knife; yes, the tree or bush looks hurt, but the result is sweeter and larger fruit and beautiful colorful roses.

> "[7] Endure hardship as discipline; God is treating you as his children. For what children are not disciplined by their father? [8] If you are not disciplined—and everyone undergoes discipline—then you are not legitimate, not true sons and daughters at all. [9] Moreover, we have

all had human fathers who disciplined us and we respected them for it. How much more should we submit to the Father of spirits and live! [10] They disciplined us for a little while as they thought best; but God disciplines us for our good, in order that we may share in his holiness. [11] No discipline seems pleasant at the time, but painful. Later on, however, it produces a harvest of righteousness and peace for those who have been trained by it." (Heb. 12:7, 11)

That's what we want, stress that contributes to peace. Good solid, hard training; no pain, no gain. When you know the end result is going to be made better it brings peace not undo pressure, it may still hurt, but you can handle it more calmly.

God may move your earth but He won't give you an earthquake. God will let some snow fall on you, but it won't be an avalanche (Phil. 4:7), "[7]And the peace of God, which transcends all understanding, will guard your hearts and your minds in Christ Jesus."

The devil wants to go beyond what God allows even using us to harm ourselves, but God "checks" him. God is trying to build us while Satan is trying to bury us. God will allow us to be pushed to the building point, but not to the breaking point. Only God knows the difference, and He filters every load of stress. I assure you (2 Cor. 12:9), [9] But he said to me, "My grace is sufficient for you, for my power is made perfect in weakness…"

God bless you,
Fwfm; nlw

The Miracles of Elisha

It's so tempting to summarize Elisha's ministry as miraculous because other than our Lord Jesus, Elisha performed the most miracles. But let's keep this in context; each miracle was the manifestation of authority and power granted by God. God wanted to show man, I'm permitting Elisha to do things no other human can do.

Secondly I'm showing the idol worshippers of that day (and there were many) that God, Yahweh, Israel's God, was greater than any of the made up gods and goddesses of Canaan.

Thirdly, Elisha's miracles are a "breakthrough" a moment in time when God reaches out of the unseen realm of eternity into time. These were thin places when folk could watch a glimpse of God, revealing something of His power, His compassion, and His love. We see God via Elisha, caring, cherishing, nourishing, nurturing, and encouraging. God is telling us, help is always within our reach when we call on Him. God uses His power for our contentment, our joy, our peace of mind and we are awed. Our hearts are filled with affection for Him.

So these little vignettes—these small tokens of God's love that Elisha was permitted to do had a reason and a purpose. No one else saw God, but they sure knew via Elisha what He looked like. How does God look via your life? Can others see Him in you, via you? Are you a stumbling block or a stepping stone?

Elisha was a protege of Elijah. He worked for him God told Elijah to anoint Elisha to succeed him (1 Kings 19:15, 16). Elijah wore a mantle which he laid on Elisha's shoulders as he worked in the field (1 Kings 19): Once that mantel was laid on him, he left the field and followed Elijah.

God told Elijah, I'm calling you home. Knowing his time was imminent; Elijah was determined to leave a strong legacy. He therefore asked his disciple, "What can I do for you before I am taken from you?"

Elijah was confident Elisha would do the right thing. What did Elisha want, hmm? (Deut. 21:17). Elisha knew he would succeed Elijah in his work, but he also knew he could not take on his responsibilities and face its perils without adequate resources. Yes, Elisha was eager to seek the Spirit that endowed the old prophet with power from on high. Elisha said, "I'm a mere man, but I serve a mighty God. Therefore I need His power to do this job."

2 Kings 2:1–12

What did he ask for preacher, he asked for a double portion of whatever Elijah had. So Elijah said, "Fine, if you see me when I am taken from you; it will be a double portion—otherwise not."

That's sounds about right doesn't it? I mean if you're going to work for God you certainly should be able to "see." So as they were walking along and talking together, suddenly a chariot of fire and horse of fire appeared and separated the two of them and Elijah went up to heaven in a whirlwind. Elisha saw this and cried out, my father! My father! The chariot and horsemen of Israel! And Elisha saw him no more.

You see Elijah's requirement that Elisha see departure had to do with one's ability to see what cannot be seen. "Elijah was a man like us" (James 5:17). This was not latent or inherent human ability, no his eyes were fixed on what is unseen (2 Cor. 4:18).

That was the secret of his influence and strength. The big test for Elisha was, have you learned the secret?

An ordinary man or woman standing in that place would have seen nothing; the sudden disappearance of the old prophet Elijah. Who knows why men are blinded from seeing the things of God? Maybe its sin, maybe its materialism, maybe it's a lack of interest in godly things, whatever the reason, no one else but Elisha saw Elijah caught up. Elisha learned from Elijah to fix his eyes on what is unseen…

And so it is with us, we need to stop looking around; to look down is to be depressed. To look around is to be distressed, but to look up is to be blessed. Look up past the clouds, look via the clouds and see Jesus. Fix your eyes…on the star post of glory.

Look past your taste, touch, sound, smell or hearing and have faith in God. Gain access to the invisible. My hope is built on nothing less… Don't let your eyes grow dim with the things of this world. Look past this old world; Paul said in Heb. 11:1, Faith is the substance of things hoped for… By faith we know the world was formed by God (Gen. 1:1)

By faith, we know that Abel offered a more excellent sacrifice than Cain. By Faith Noah built an Ark…by faith Abraham was told to look for a city whose builder and maker was God. By faith, ninety-year-old Sarah conceived and was with child. By faith Moses refused to be called the son of Pharaoh and rather chose to suffer affliction with the people of God than to enjoy the pleasures of sin for a season. By faith Moses took the children of Israel from the bondage of Egypt and as they stood before what looked like an impossible dream, he dared to raise his staff…

Mountains on one side, desert on the other, Pharaoh's army behind him, and the Red Sea stood before him. Moses saw the power of God when no one else could see it… God opened up that Red Sea… By faith Joshua stood at the walls of Jericho…(song), he marched around that wall for seven days and…

By faith, Rahab the harlot didn't perish with the city because she saw God in the two spies Joshua sent and hid these in her house (Josh 2).

You see without faith it's impossible to please God. The songwriter said, "Where is your faith in God?"

Faith just can't be generated; it's a gift of God given as an answer to prayer. Do you want to see God in all His glory? Then pray that your eyes would be opened, and that your heart may be enlightened. Song: "Open My Eyes That I May See."

Faith grows as we feed on God's Word. Faith comes by hearing the Word (Rom. 10:17). If you would be spiritually aware and see everything via God's eyes, then you've got to get into His Word. You must be born again, again.

Faith is a product of obedience. What do you see preacher: It depends on what kind of person you are. Matthew 5:8 said, "The pure in heart shall see God." But preacher what do you see?

I see trees of green, red roses too
I see them bloom for me and you
And I think to myself what a wonderful world.

I see skies of blue and clouds of white
The bright blessed day, the dark sacred night
And I think to myself what a wonderful world.

The colors of the rainbow so pretty in the sky
Are also on the faces of people going by
I see friends shaking hands saying how do you do
They're really saying I love you.

I hear babies cry, I watch them grow
They'll learn much more than I'll never know
And I think to myself what a wonderful world
Yes I think to myself what a wonderful world.

I see better marriages. I see better families. I see families staying together, praying together, and eating together. I see folks reaching out to others no matter what color they are or where they came from, saying God loves you and so do I.

I don't see that preacher… Maybe you don't see it because you're not ready to see it. Maybe you don't see it because your devotion to Christ is contaminated by the world. My God told me if I can perceive it I can achieve it.

Come on, Elisha, do another miracle, show the world God. No! My time is past, but how about you; you do one, why don't you just testify…testimony: poverty, projects, broken home, bad marriages all around me, but…

Song: It Took a Miracle

My Father is omnipotent
And that you can't deny
A Wonder working miracles
You can see it in the sky.

It took a miracle
To put the world into place
It took a miracle
To put the stars into space

But when He saved my soul
Cleansed and made me whole
It was a miracle
Of love and grace!

It took a miracle
to hang the moon in the sky
It took a miracle
To put Heaven on high

But when He saved my soul
Cleansed and made me whole
It was a miracle
of love and pure grace.

Song: I Need Thee Every Hour...
Just As I Am

If you've never seen a miracle, take a good look
at me...
If it had not been for the Lord on my side...

God bless you,
Fwfm: nlw

What Season is it in Your Life?

Ecclesiastes 3:1

We all understand the seasons; we have lived through enough of them to be quite familiar with each one. The cold wetness of winter. The sunny brightness of spring with everything growing and turning green. Then the warmth of Summer, oh the fruits, so colorful, and then comes Autumn or Fall, and what was once green turns yellow, red, then brown and finally falls down to either be picked up or blown away by the wind; wow, the seasons.

Did you know we also have seasons in our lives? The spring of new things, new jobs, new relationships, new marriages, new babies. Then the warm summer of travel and swimming, the long days, and warm nights, walking in cool of the evening; fall comes and there goes that relationship, there goes that job, the children are back in school, not soon enough. Winter comes and we lose a close friend or relative.

Yes, the seasons of life are real. Some of us don't recover from life's winters. We lose a friend or relative and spring may come for others, but we're trapped in winter; dark, cold, wet, heavy winter.

Well, God wants to make sure we're aware that for everything there is a season. However, unlike earth's seasons, our hearts or life's seasons do not come in any particular order. They also come without warning or logic, they must happen. We don't know how long they are going to stay or if they are just passing through. At least with the other seasons of the world they have a cycle of order, and we can prepare.

So what then do we do preacher, to deal with the seasons of our lives? Wouldn't it be nice if we could be evergreens…always bearing leaves no matter what season? That is so special. Does that have anything to do with our spiritual maturity or is it more just our general personality and makeup?

Jesus told us to bear much fruit to glorify God, so He must have been talking about seasons to produce good fruit? They need winter's dormancy, spring's flourishing, summer's basking, and fall's ripeness.

Each season has a reason, a beauty, and a danger. You have to be careful not to under estimate either one. Each season may be integral or get an assist in growing the fruit but only one of them is going to make the basket or reap the fruit.

So we should not fret over so many changes in our lives, it's all a part of the seasons. Just use a little discernment, don't plant flowers in January. Don't pull flowers in July or prime trees in May; neither do you till soil in November. You don't harvest oranges in summer; pick the appropriate season to do these things.

When it comes to people, you don't know what they're going through, how can you judge them? Why are your expectations so high for them? You don't know what season it is in their life? Let's not concentrate on others, let's try to figure out what time it is in our own life.

Have we missed the parallel to our own spirit? Why am I trying to sow new seed in the winter of my life? I can't let people coax me into busy, busy, busy, when I just lost my job, marriage, relative. No wonder I'm depleted, I haven't even healed fully yet; I haven't recovered from moving or my other issues. I've had three winters in a row, no wonder I feel exhausted. This isn't the time in my life to plant seed to do new things, this is the time to cut back and take a retrospective view. This is the time to fertilize, to prepare for the spring I'm praying God sends soon.

If it's spring in my life, I ought to be busy enjoying it, not sitting around brooding and idle. This is a time for opportunity while I'm feeling real good. All these stirrings in my soul, I need to make some things happen. I need to be on and cracking.

Recognize your season folks and work it accordingly and leave other folks alone. To everything there is a season. This one woman named Sharon and her husband Richard, were "church folk." Their family was raised in the church. They met in the church. His mother taught Sunday school and her father was the SS superintendent. They were equally yoked. Beautiful family with two kids, it was just spring seasonably speaking. Youth groups met at the house, beautiful vacations, wow!

Then the season just abruptly changed, Fall came. Richard was caught cheating and confessed to a pattern of repeated infidelities stretching all the way back to the start of their marriage. It was fall going into a cold dark Winter… (come on, put your big coat on).

Richard ran off leaving Sharon to deal with the trauma of this awful discovery and the kids. Sharon still comes to church, but most Sunday's she just sits alone in the back. She resigned from all positions in the church and is just trying to recover.

But here comes the church folk. What's wrong with Sharon, She doesn't seem like herself; she's so quiet. Other folk are just singing so loud and boisterous, she remembers when she and Richard used to sing that way… As all the words seemed so unreal, someone had the nerve to say Sharon doesn't even sing like she used to.

Sharon, overhearing this said, "How can I, those words aren't working for me anymore. How about somebody put a tune to Psalms 88, that I could sing?"

No, that wouldn't be a good song people. The fact is, every church is full of Sharon's…trying to figure who they are now, and where God is in their dark Winter. They are wondering if God knows the city they live in, if He knows their zip code? Unfortunately so many Sharon's did not know (Eccles. 3:1).

Yes, it's real, yes, this season is well trod, charted waters and the Man of sorrows is quite familiar with it (Isa. 53). Sharon doesn't need a pill, or alcohol; she doesn't need a pep talk; neither does she need to get busy. Sharon needs to understand (Eccles. 3:1) and God will carry you and strengthen you when you're weak. He will build you up when you're torn down, and prop you up on every leaning side.

It may be winter now, but weeping may endure for a night, but joy cometh in the morning. Recognize your season and work it accordingly. There is a rhythm to it like kayaking. You've got to know when to row together forward and when to coast.

During your winter just coast. As it warms up a little, get into some things as the Lord leads you. Don't you flap around in winter because you ain't going anywhere, you're just flapping. When spring arrives get busy; talk to some folk... In your summer, bask, enjoy, travel, touch lives, and let somebody touch your life.

In your fall gather the fruit, bring in the sheaves (dinner parties, youth sports, etc.) Enjoy what you've planted that has now grown. Then as Winter approaches again, cut back some more busyness, prune again, plant and prepare. Don't let your winter be too dark, too cold, and too muddy. Don't let your spring be too windy to lush with leaves and flowers so you lose yourself. Don't let your Summer be too hot and parched or your Fall too barren. Work your seasons—walk with God, talk with God...

God bless you,
Fwfm: nlw

The Results of Trust and Obedience

Believers must trust God. It's kind of hard to obey a God whom you don't trust. Wouldn't you agree that the majority of disobedience occurs when a believer says, "I know what the Lord says, but...?" Anytime we put a "but" at the end of something God said we are about to come up with an excuse, a justification, or a rationalization to disobey.

We must know and acknowledge who God is. When we do this and mull His sovereignty, goodness, love, mercy, grace, kindness and etc. over and over in our heads, how can we but trust Him. Either God is who He says He is, does what He says He does, or He's a fake, an imposter. Well, we know beyond a shadow of a doubt God is no fake, so then why do we insist on disobeying. It's a lack of trusting and all-loving God; go ahead and admit it.

The sooner you do, the sooner you can drop the excuses and honor God for who He is. No matter who we are obedience equals blessings while doubt and disobedience leads to sorrow and misery.

We can depend on God, He has never failed us. He is the winning team. Wouldn't it be better to walk beside Him than to resist His love and care and efforts to steer us in the right direction? So here is my question, are you going to trust God and obey for the new year and progress or are you going to do your own thing and regress back into the previous year and backwards? If you're sticking with the old, how's that working for you?

God bless you,
Fwfm: nlw

Precipice Warnings

A precipice is a slippery slope. It is also a situation of great peril. It is the face of a cliff; also the brink of a dangerous or disastrous situation. Why then do we literally play around these "slippery slopes"? It's almost like watching a movie or real life of someone doing something extremely dangerous and foolish and instead of learning from it we long to try it. Suddenly, bam! There goes the slide, which was predictable for all who play near a precipice.

We have all heard the term "slippery slopes." The whole idea or thought of this makes any wise person think caution or danger ahead. Anyone who willingly or deliberately ignores real danger is on a "slippery slope." Jeremiah 23:12 said, "Therefore their way will be like slippery paths to them, They will be driven away into the gloom and fall down in it; For I will bring calamity upon them, The year of their punishment," declares the LORD." There is such a thing as a precipice of darkness. You can't just decide to do whatever you want when you want and everyone else and everything else be damned. You find out sooner than later who really gets damned.

Those who willfully climb over the guard rails and fences of moral and spiritual warnings place themselves on a slippery slope. We don't ever want to say, "They deserved it because we know the moral cravings we all have. What we want to do is say like in Galatians 6:10: "Dear brothers and sisters, if another believer is overcome by some sin, you who are godly should gently and humbly help that person back onto the right path. And be careful not to fall into the same temptation yourself." Whether or not it was foolish is immaterial; let's let God be the judge and meanwhile do our best to stay off of the slippery slopes.

We must change our behavior to avoid the slippery slopes as opposed to playing on them. What is our attraction to them, what is our affinity to them? It's like we are gambling with our life, our emotions, and our spirit. This is not a time to play with danger, tossing out wisdom. The precipice of darkness is unkind to all who venture its way. It's waiting for you to get too close and bam!

God bless you,
Fwfm; nlw

When All Else Is Gone

Too many people are being backed into a corner today. The odds are seemingly stacked against them. They have lost so much it seems like there is nothing else to lose. When you get to this point in life when all else is gone, hold on to Jesus; no one can take Him away from you.

This world (cosmos) we live in is not our home. It is not friendly. It will take and take and take. What it cannot take is the joy Jesus gives us down in our soul despite the circumstances. It doesn't matter the reason adversity has moved in with us. All we know is it wasn't enough that calamity was our next-door neighbor; now adversity is rooming with us.

I can tell you this, when you look at the biblical record when kings who knew God were pushed to the wall, they all did the same thing. They fasted and prayed and asked God for deliverance in His own way.

Remember King Jehoshaphat in 2 Chronicles 19:20 It happened after this: This threat to Jehoshaphat and his kingdom happened after his return to seeking God following his near death when he allied himself with king Ahab of Israel.

The people of Moab with the people of Ammon, and others with them besides the Ammonites, came to battle against Jehoshaphat: This great multitude was a significant threat against Jehoshaphat, whose last experience on the field of battle was a narrow escape from death.

Jehoshaphat feared: There was certainly a sense in which Jehoshaphat feared the great multitude coming against him. Yet the sense here is that he feared the LORD, and was more awed at the power and majesty of God than at the destructive force of his enemies.

This is a recurring theme in 2 Chronicles: for leaders who seek the LORD. We can expect God to do great things when His people, and especially the leaders of His people, seek Him. Others who sought the LORD in 2 Chronicles include the following:

- The faithful remnant of Israel (2 Chronicles 11:16)
- The people of Judah under king Asa (2 Chronicles 14:4, 15:12–13)
- Jehoshaphat in the early part of his reign (2 Chronicles 19:3)
- King Hezekiah (2 Chronicles 31:21)
- King Josiah (2 Chronicles 34:3)

His attitude is summed up by the word *seek*, which occurs twice in Hebrew though it is variously translated.... This is a key word in Jehoshaphat's reign, where it has the basic sense of 'worship', but also means to discover God's will. It shows that Jehoshaphat has a higher trust in God than in his military resources."

He proclaimed a fast throughout all Judah: Jehoshaphat called the nation to express their humility and total dependence upon God through a public fast—that is, abstaining from all food for a period of time (typically a day or more) and drinking only water.

When all else is gone you learn to trust God. He will not fail you. It may not be the answer you want but it will be an answer you need and will help you.

It was no different with Gideon in Judges 7:1–7. He went from thirty-two thousand men to three hundred to fight over a million-man army. When all else is gone you learn to trust God.

We have to learn to trust God even in dire circumstances. Everything is not always going to work in our favor and anyone who tells you it is they are not being honest or truthful with you. Be careful of listening to televangelists making you promises that the Bible does not back.

Just because you go via a multitude of problems does not mean God has abandoned you. When you lose a job, lose a marriage, lose a friend or lose a loved one; it's not over. Stand your ground, stay focused and ascertain that when all else fails you will always still have God. Let Him lead you via the darkness to the marvelous light.

God bless you,
Fwfm; nlw

Lord, I'm Suffering; You Can't Just Take Me?

Job 3–7

Job has undergone severe testing, completely unaware that he is the subject of a challenge between God and Satan. All he knows is there has been one calamity after another and he is in horrible agony. He lost all of his ten kids, his wife turned against him, and he lost all his possessions. To top it off he has a dreadful disease that has disfigured him. He is in such bad shape his own wife urges him to curse God and destroy himself. Yet despite it all Job still trust in God's mercy and love. He flat out resists the devil and his wife.

Job makes it clear, God is good, and His love endures forever. If He allows extreme discomfort and agony to come into our lives, He does so for reasons beyond our finite understanding and that are good and perfect, and loving.

Job 3:1–10

These are extreme emotions, the result of extreme agony. Have you ever felt that way? Just wish you could hide somewhere or drop off the face of the earth, just go home and be with Jesus; where the wicked cease from troubling...

This is what Job was feeling and God wanted us to know because when our turn comes He wanted us to be ready, and not feeling helpless. So He told Job, write this down... God sometimes leads or allow us into places of discomfort and agony, where we feel downright helpless. Once we're there we find Jesus is our only alternative, our only relief.

Job was so troubled he came close to cursing God but he never crossed the line. Few things are harder to bear than meaningless suffering. Lord, if we just knew why we're going through this thick jungle of anguish… Perhaps that would make it easier to endure. (I was a good H/W…), but bad things happen to good people. So Job cried out in misery, why was I even born? My only relief is to go home to God and be with my Lord.

Verses 11, 12

Then without any knowledge of the Bible look at Jobs view of death.

Verses 13–19

A time of rest, a period of solitude and quiet after a life of trouble…that's what you call limited understanding. God makes sure by the time this book ends Job comes into complete accuracy…

Next Job approaches a question a whole lot of folk ask today; why doesn't God just take me home so I wouldn't have to go via all this suffering?

Verses 20–26

What is the purpose of my life? What use is a life so full of misery? I mean look at me, why can't this old worn frame just give out, it's no good anyway? Why do I have to endure or prolong the agony?

So then as if you're not in enough pain, three of his alleged closest friends drop by to offer comfort… Eliphaz tries to be elegant (smooth, polished). Bildad, he is just plain brutal and frank. Zophar, he attempts to be zealous, emotional and compassionate but it's not only what you say, but also how you say it; but, what you say still matters. E. G. (notification, divorce, etc.).

Eliphaz starts out; notice how elegant he sounds in 4:2–6: "Job, you've been a counselor to a lot of people and you were able to help them solve their problems. You helped them face the truth about their own hurts; now you need to follow that same advice. You've been caught up in something and struck down by it now you're feeling discouraged. If you're truly innocent why do you feel so bad; be confident that you've done no wrong."

Then he goes on the attack in verses 7–11.

Lions describe the natural strength of humans. He says evil man may appear strong, but in God's judging hand his power is broken. In other words, the righteous are never punished; only the unrighteous suffer. Did you ever see an innocent man perish? Only the unrighteous man suffers. Evil men don't succeed. This is subtle, this is elegant?

Job is accused here of hiding sin in his life (if you're suffering you must have sinned, because these sorts of things don't happen to upright, innocent people) there's something wrong with your life Job. So that's it, that's comfort?

These are extreme evangelicals who love to judge others. The reason Dr. Billy Graham is sick is this is God's judgment against him for associating with the wrong kinds of people. The reason Pres. Obama needed stitches in his lip is because God was sending him a warning against his policies; there are things he needed to sew up.

One of these type fellas fell down a flight of stairs and broke his leg and was reduced to hobbling around on crutches. His explanation for his injury was that Satan was attacking him and trying to stop his ministry for God. How typical of these types; when it's someone else their troubles are caused by their sin, but when it's them they're been attacked by Satan trying to halt their wonderful work they are doing for the Lord; isn't that special? How self-deceived can you be?

Verses 12–17

Eliphaz says he was visited in the middle of the night by a spirit interrupting his dreams and waking him up. You sure this wasn't a horror film. This thing came to his face filling him with fear and trembling, making the hair on his body stand up and causing his bones to shake. This thing spoke in a hushed whisper voice. It gave this impression that it spoke for God, but it never says I'm from God. So Eliphaz assumes and would have Job to believe this was an angel? But that's funny; angels in the scripture don't usually behave this way.

In Genesis 18, Abraham welcomed three angels who appeared to be human travelers. In Genesis 19, two angels went to Sodom as human visitors. In Mark 16, a young man was dressed in a white robe; clearly Eliphaz visitor didn't fit any of these descriptions.

Not only so the sudden appearance of an angel was often startling and when people were frightened by an angel, the angel always said, "fear not, or do not be afraid." You remember Hagar in Genesis 21:17, Elijah in 2 Kings 1:15, Joseph in Matthew 1:20, Virgin Mary in Luke 1:30, Zechariah, the father of John the Baptist in Luke 1:13, the Shepherds in Luke 2:8–11, and the women at the garden tomb in Mark 16:6. Each one of the angels had the same character and mannerisms saying, "Fear not." So we have to believe whatever this was that visited Eliphaz was not from God.

And the message in verses 17–21:

Talking about humans "those who live in houses of clay whose foundation is in the dust" houses being our bodies. This use of metaphorical language is meant to demean human beings. This spirit thing asks, "does a human have the right to question God?" No, so no right to ask for anything either. We're insignificant, we're fragile as moths. Humanity is beneath God's notice.

Now we have no doubt this was an evil spirit pretending to be an angel of God. A true messenger of God would never portray God as indifferent to people and consider humans unworthy. Everywhere in the scriptures God loves His people and takes care of them. Luke 12:7 said He loves us so much that He has numbered the hairs on our heads. How about Psalm 23?

Did you also notice this when this minion that visited Eliphaz seems to complain about God's judgment against fallen angels—the demons who followed Satan in his rebellion?

"God places no trust in His servants and that He charges His angles with error." This is the sort of complaint Satan himself might make against God. These demons were undoubtedly baffled and resented over the fact that God actually loves these miserable little creatures that live from dusk to dawn whose bodies are made of dust.

Eliphaz actually believes he has been privileged to receive an oracle from God. He has no clue that this message was given to him by the evil one as a means of attacking and undermining Job. So Eliphaz repeats his argument: God is infinite; human beings are nothing. If the angels can't stand, do you really believe humans have a chance? No mention of love, compassion, forgiveness, and patience—you know, all the attributes of God.

So basically no matter how Eliphaz dresses it with half truths his message is an unbalanced lie. This is how so much error gets into the doctrine of evangelicals. We cite the scripture in support of our doctrinal beliefs yet our beliefs are false or incomplete; so we turn God's truth into an ugly falsehood.

Job 5:1–4

What a low blow. Without saying it directly Eliphaz insults Job and calls him a fool. (E. G. when Doc called me a fool…) (Like a plant taking root in good, well-watered soil, became wealthy and prosperous; roots in the Bible generally refer to strength, health, wealth and a flourishing life).

Eliphaz, did you envy Job? What is this cruel reference to the calamity that befell all Job's children in one day? The house of this fool was cursed and his children exposed to danger, then crushed?

Why did all this happen, Job, because you have sin in your life? (Satan does not play fair.) "Trouble just doesn't spring from the ground it has a cause…" (Job 5:5–7). This is flawed theology, the whole fifth chapter.

If you have lived long at all you know godly people are not exempt from trouble. In fact the Word says we will go via trials and suffering because they are godly (2 Tim. 3:12). It's a fairy tale to think you're exempt from trials if you're a believer. This book of Job was written to correct such errors in our theology. Of course we suffer for sin many times, but always for living a righteous life.

Job's Response (6:2–4)

I have a right to complain…, my sorrow is terrible. If you were where I am, you'd understand.

Verses 8–13

Job says, Lord what do you think I'm made of, stone or bronze? I've reached my limit of endurance. Lord you promised to never go beyond what I could bear, but we passed that weeks ago.
(E. G. Bow and arrow from Oswald Chambers)

Verses 22, 23

Did I ask you to help me? I didn't send for you or your comfort. Please don't do me any favors

Verses 24–30

My life may not be sinless but I've kept short accounts with God, quickly confessing my wrong (7:19–21).

Have you ever felt that way? Please Lord, I'm suffering; you can't just take me home?
No more, I've had enough. Keep in mind Job does not know what we know. We caught a glimpse of the purpose for Job's suffering that he hasn't seen.
Something to keep in mind for us; every time you go via some trial and suffering there are two purposes in view. Satan will use any kind of agony, illness, or whatever, to torment, including alleged well-intentioned but misguided friends who claim to be bringing comfort but are instead inflicting cruelty. Then he takes God's silence to assault us and drive in the wedge to break our faith.

But this is what God will do:

1. He will help us whether we can see it or not.
2. He will teach us and grow us via the trial.
3. We will get to understand deep and profound things via our suffering…
4. God will teach Satan and all powers and principalities; listen, you're wrong, you were wrong from the beginning when you first fell and you're wrong still. Not only so, don't mess with my children (Eph. 3:10, 11).
5. All of our suffering is woven into this vast eternal purpose of God which he accomplished via our Lord Jesus. Each time we're afflicted God provides a massive demonstration for all the heavenly powers that "My judgment is real, My judgment is fair; My ways are perfect, there's a reason you're still here (E. G., *It's a Wonderful Life with Jimmy Stewart*). One of these great getting up morning we will fly away, but until then…

God bless you,
Fwfm; nlw

The Christian Life Journey

Is it going to be our way or God's way? That is the question. Will the new year be just like the past year or will we submit, truly submit? Have we finalized our next move or are we still relying on other people?

There is only one way to live the Christian life and that is by obedience to God. Does that sound boring to you? It shouldn't? We serve a wonderfully creative God who knows all the twists and turns our life will take. If God's answer concerning some prayer is no not today, then you can be sure there is another avenue he has for us to travel.

Our life in the new year comes down to one question; how much do we trust God? If we have perfect trust in Him, we will let go of our need to control whatever we are facing and allow him to guide us through each moment. F. B. Meyer said, "Dread not any result of implicit obedience to God's for command; fear not the angry waters which, in their proud insolence forbid your progress."

Above the voices of many waters, the mighty breakers of the sea, the Lord sitteth King forever… Dare to trust him; dare to follow him and discover that the very forces which barred your progress and threatened your very existence, at His bidding become the materials of which an avenue is made to liberty.

Whether it is a decision that must be made or a problem that must be faced, faith in God's creative love for you is the answer. Be willing to trust Him for the outcome as you acknowledge His greatness and sovereignty in your life. Then rest in the knowledge that he is in control of all things. What a mighty God we serve.

[28] We are confident that God is able to orchestrate everything to work toward something good and beautiful when we love Him and accept His invitation to live according to His plan. (Rom. 8:28, The Voice).

God bless you,
Fwfm; nlw

How Precious Is Our Faith?

God has made so many promises to us since the foundation of this world. I like the way Jeremiah described it in Lamentations,

21 This I recall to my mind, therefore have I hope. 22 It is of the Lord's mercies that we are not consumed, because his compassions fail not.

> 23 They are new every morning: great is thy faithfulness.
> 24 The Lord is my portion, saith my soul; therefore will I hope in him.

God's Word to us is revealing His heart to us. This is how precious our faith is. It is not about anything we have done for Him, it is all because of what He has done for us (John 3:16). Our whole faith is based on God's great promises. Just look at what Peter said.

> 1 Simon Peter, a servant and an apostle of Jesus Christ, to them that have obtained like precious faith with us through the righteousness of God and our Saviour Jesus Christ:
> 2 Grace and peace be multiplied unto you through the knowledge of God, and of Jesus our Lord,
> 3 According as his divine power hath given unto us all things that pertain unto life and godliness, through the knowledge of him that hath called us to glory and virtue:
> 4 Whereby are given unto us exceeding great and precious promises: that by these ye might be par-

takers of the divine nature, having escaped the corruption that is in the world through lust.

⁵ And beside this, giving all diligence, add to your faith virtue; and to virtue knowledge;

⁶ And to knowledge temperance; and to temperance patience; and to patience godliness;

⁷ And to godliness brotherly kindness; and to brotherly kindness charity.

⁸ For if these things be in you, and abound, they make you that ye shall neither be barren nor unfruitful in the knowledge of our Lord Jesus Christ.

⁹ But he that lacketh these things is blind, and cannot see afar off, and hath forgotten that he was purged from his old sins.

If you believe your faith to be precious and you should; do you want more and more of God's kindness and peace? Then you have to learn to know him better and better. The more you know about the attributes of God, He will give you power through the Holy Spirit.

Everything you need for living a truly good life God will grant it and more. For instance; the promise to save us from the lust and rottenness all around us, and to give us his own character, that is how precious we are to God. He knows without his help we do not have a chance.

But to obtain these gifts, you need more than faith; it takes hard work and study of God's Word to be good and even that is not enough. For then you must learn to know God better and discover what he wants you to do. Then we have to learn to put aside our own desires so that we will become patient and godly, gladly letting God have his way with us.

This is what makes the next step possible which is for you to enjoy other people and to like them; we all know how hard that can be. Finally you will grow to love them with God to help. The more we trust God and lean on him, the more we will grow strong spiritually and become fruitful and useful to our Lord Jesus Christ.

We already know what happens to the others to fail to listen and want to do their own thing; just look around at all the churches; no changes. Listen, this is for folks who know how precious their faith is and want a life-changing experience. God is a straight shooter; this is intervention at its best.

We have been invited to join the best and forsake the rest; we cannot afford to squander this invitation. Let's take everything God is offering and use it to our advantage. Then when the trials of life beat down on us we are prepared to stand. Listen to what the song writer said.

1. Standing on the promises of Christ my King,
   Through eternal ages let His praises ring,
   Glory in the highest, I will shout and sing,
   Standing on the promises of God.
   o Refrain:
   Standing, standing,
   Standing on the promises of God my Savior;
   Standing, standing,
   I'm standing on the promises of God.

2. Standing on the promises that cannot fail,
   When the howling storms of doubt and fear assail,
   By the living Word of God I shall prevail,
   Standing on the promises of God.

God bless you,
Fwfm; nlw

Choice to Change

Everybody is talking about a new beginning and change because it is a New Year. Do we really need to wait for New Years before improvement happens? God made us with mind, free will, and intellect. At any given time we could alter our being. We can choose right, left, up, down, whatever we believe to be best.

God has specifically asked us to rid ourselves of all offenses we have committed and get a new heart and a new spirit (Ezek. 18:31). [31] Cast away from you all your transgressions, whereby ye have transgressed; and make you a new heart and a new spirit: for why will ye die, O house of Israel? Not only so but the word repent is spoken of throughout the Bible. Turn away from sin; how many times have we heard this?

You see it is all about choices. We can either be led by the Spirit or we can choose to lead ourselves. We must stop listening to people who claim God is far away or far off. God is as close as we want him to be. [9] The Lord is not slack concerning his promise, as some men count slackness; but is longsuffering to us-ward, not willing that any should perish, but that all should come to repentance (2 Pet. 3:9).

> [32] For I have no pleasure in the death of him that dieth, saith the Lord God: wherefore turn yourselves, repent and live. Our God can take a heart of stone and make it flesh. God will give us a spiritual heart transplant if we want it. Nothing will be forced on us; we have to want change for the better.

Do you want the new year to be the same as past years or do you want change for the better; the choice is yours?

God bless you,
Fwfm; nlw

Walking by Faith

It's a little difficult isn't it to break our normal pattern? We have been perceiving the world via sight, smell, hearing, taste, and touch for our way of gaining any information we needed to function. Now God introduces us to this thing called faith. The evidence of things not seen yet we are supposed to believe. God is telling us there is truth beyond what you can see or touch or feel or hear; wow! What is this truth Lord, show me. God then says I will not show you, just trust me; okay, this isn't easy.

God not only tells us about faith but He demands that we have it. Those that would come to Him must come by faith. They must believe that He is; and that He is a rewarder of them that diligently seek Him (Heb. 11:6). When we depend on God it's not blind faith, it's not our opinion or circumstances or feelings, it's a gift from God which we have no control over (Eph. 2:8). So those who would have faith or have their faith strengthened, we need but ask and God will grant it.

How preacher, how do we walk by faith and not by sight? It's simple, we live like we believe, we sing like we believe, we give like we believe and every decision we make we act like we believe God. He then rewards us for our actions and behavior based on our faith and His grace.

Does this mean we will not have trials, no, we will have trials, but we also use our faith via these and God will assist us? He may remove them, or He may walk with us via them; either way we are made stronger and better and our faith in God increases.

God sent the Holy Spirit to lead, guide and direct us; all we have to do is follow by faith. He will give us wisdom, knowledge, and encouragement. He will be a lamp unto our feet and a light unto our pathway. All direction will be handled via and by Him; we just have to have the faith to follow.

He will meet our needs; He knows what is best for us and He will provide. Yes, we will fall down, but He will help us up and start us off again with a new and fresh slate. When we veer off track God's forgiveness and grace move our repentant heart back in gear. The more we trust Him, the deeper our relationship becomes. The more we lean on Him and focus on Him our faith increases.

Listen, it's not about us handling life on our own. Why even try, God has shown us a better and necessary way—faith in Him. He will never leave us or forsake us (Heb. 13:5, 6). He will never let us down or fail us. He is not a man that He should lie (Num. 23:19). So why do we allow life to stress us and overwhelm us when we could simply trust God whose record is impeccable?

Oh, the rest and peace He brings even in the midst of troubles and sorrow. Believers smile and have a sense of confidence coming from them even in the worst circumstances, why? It's because we know God has the ultimate say and He sees what we cannot and He will work it out.

Our wise omnipotent, omnipresent, omnicious God and Father which art in heaven; hallowed be thy name. Why, because He's working it out, because He's sovereign, because He is supreme. The devil is mighty but he is not almighty. The devil is powerful but he is not all powerful. Oh but our God is an awesome God, He reigns… Every time we go via something and we trust God He builds our confidence; He increases our desire to walk by faith.

In those times and days, when we struggle to trust and believe, we have to just remember to relinquish control to Him. He didn't bring us this far to leave us. Don't start trying to take matters into your own hands because you hit a snag. God is patient and loving and just because you fall down doesn't mean you're through. The songwriter said, "We fall down, but we get back up again. A saint is just someone who fell down but got back up." You only fail when you stay down.

We're in the process of being sanctified. Sanctification doesn't happen overnight. God demands holiness, but He also helps us become holy. Just keep walking by faith and step by step we're walking closer and closer to God.

God is trying to tell us there is so much more to life than our senses. Ain't nothing wrong with our senses but a man/woman of faith God takes to higher planes. All we have to do is have a willing mind and a willing heart ready to learn and receive and God will teach us things we could only imagine and some things we cannot even dream. Oh, what a mighty God we serve.

The more we trust Him the more we grow strong and the better our choices. The Spirit of God will take us to heights unknown. Eyes have not seen, ears have not heard what God can do. He'll do for you what no other man or woman can do. The Word said oh taste and see the God is good...

God bless you,
Fwfm; nlw

The Peace of God

In order to have peace we have to let go of the things that weigh us down. We also have to put things in perspective in our lives. What would God have me do with this? We are allowing too many things to interfere with our peace; things like fear and anxiety. This is the reason God kept having the angels repeat over and over again "fear not" in so many instances.

We are prone to fear and it damages or blocks our peace. God has promised us peace so we have to believe it and receive it. We cannot allow anxious thoughts to creep into our minds and dominate our thinking. We must not lay awake at night stressing over concerns we should have submitted to God in prayer.

John 14:27, 16:33

We have to put it in gear; a vehicle can't move unless you put it in gear. We are designed for peace not worry. The Hebrew word for peace is "shalom" which also means "hello or goodbye." Shalom is fullness, wholeness, completeness, abundance, safety—pretty much life as God intended for us before the fall. We originally had a Garden of Eden sense of well-being.

Jesus was called our Prince of Peace, which refers to shalom, the One who fulfills us, makes us whole, and gives us hope. Every area of our life is affected by the love of Christ. None of it includes worry and fret, discontent and emptiness. We have so much to be thankful for. We cannot only rest in what God has done, but what He is doing and continues to do in our lives; this brings peace.

In this love of Christ, there is no manipulation, striving, addiction or life-sapping dysfunction that grinds us like a wine-presser mashing grapes.

No, it's a worry-free zone, in fact we are told to be anxious for nothing. Yes we'll have our trials and troubles, but we have Jesus to share them with. He will go via them with us not only so, we can depend on Him, He is completely trustworthy. His words are not empty. What we need to do is transfer the truth we know in our heads to our hearts and live in peace.

God bless you,
Fwfm: nlw

The Results of Trust and Obedience

Believers must trust God. It's kind of hard to obey a God whom you don't trust. Wouldn't you agree that the majority of disobedience occurs when a believer says, "I know what the Lord says, but...?" Anytime we put a "but" at the end of something God said we are about to come up with an excuse, a justification, or a rationalization to disobey.

We must know and acknowledge who God is. When we do this and mull His sovereignty, goodness, love, mercy, grace, kindness, and etc. over and over in our heads, how can we but trust Him. Either God is who He says He is, does what He says He does, or He's a fake, an imposter. Well, we know beyond a shadow of a doubt God is no fake, so then why do we insist on disobeying. It's a lack trusting and all-loving God, go ahead and admit it.

The sooner you do, the sooner you can drop the excuses and honor God for who He is. No matter who we are obedience equals blessings while doubt and disobedience leads to sorrow and misery.

We can depend on God, He has never failed us. He is the winning team. Wouldn't it be better to walk beside Him than to resist His love and care and efforts to steer us in the right direction? So here is my question, are you going to trust God and obey for the new year and progress or are you going to do your own thing and regress back into old year. If you're sticking with the old, how's that working for you?

God bless you,
Fwfm: nlw

Wandering in the Wilderness

Can you imagine being thrown from a moving train; think of the injuries; now imagine that you're also in the middle of nowhere, stranded, and dazed?

Do you remember where you were last time bad news came?

Your position has been eliminated.

The tumor is malignant.

Your mother and I are getting a divorce.

Your dad has had a heart attack; I need you to come to the hospital.

Grandma had a stroke; you should get here as soon as possible, they don't expect her to make it.

I just don't love you anymore; I mean I love you, but I'm not in love with you.

With a single-type sentence like these, we can suddenly find ourselves dazed as if we've been thrown off a train. Suddenly we're in a dark new world; we're wandering in the wilderness. We're hurled into a new dimension; divorced, unemployed, a valley of grieving, chemo, nursing home, or suddenly single.

This is not one of our more confident or faith filled moments. I mean, we will no doubt regain our composure and balance, but for right now we're reeling; we've lost our footing. We are between, "I have no idea where I am," "I'm in a land between," and "I'm wandering in the wilderness."

If this is the "new normal," I'm lost. I don't know where I am or where I'm going. I need "spiritual on star." I know I'm supposed to keep the faith while I'm on this new journey to wherever, but it's so difficult, so dark.

Let's think about those Israelites wandering in the desert; this presented some unique challenges. At the same time with faith, there were some unique opportunities to accompany these tough transitions.

Yes, this was undesired, many of our seasons come at undesired times, times when we least expect them. Things happen to us at some of the most inopportune times.

We can identify with these children of Israel they literally went via hell and high water. Suddenly delivered from four hundred years of slavery and now making their way to the Promised Land, Canaan, but their journey is hardly straightforward—in fact, they are traveling in circles for forty years.

In Numbers 11, it's been two years now that they have been marching in this hot dusty desert, wandering in this wilderness; Things are not going well. When you're out of work for a while you get grumpy. When you're suddenly without a husband or wife one tends to get a little bitter. God may be sustaining you, but this is all new to you, different.

God was providing "manna," it arrived daily with the morning dew, so they were not hungry; they simply got tired of this "new food." It was drudgery to them to be reduced to eating the same thing day in and day out, week after week.

It literally turned into riotous complaint (Numbers 11:5, 6). Waves of disappointment flooded the camp. Grumbling spread from tent to tent, and family to family. "If only we had meat to eat!" Oh, they moaned, "We remember the fish we ate in Egypt at no cost— and the cucumbers, melons, leeks, onions and garlic; but now we have lost our appetite, we never see anything but this manna" (verses 4–6, NIV).

Can you hear the longing for what was familiar, known, and predictable? We don't like this cafeteria food… What have you done to us, we're weary, we were better off in slavery. We were better off without you.

Now before we criticize the children of Israel for their ingratitude and ungratefulness, let's take an introspective view of our own lives. It's easy to criticize them but what about some of our complaints while we travel the "land between" or the "wilderness road"? Let's examine our own and hear what we have been complaining about.

What is eroding our energy and draining our joy? What is causing this choir of discontent to swell up and say, "We're sick of this...?" Is it possible that our voice is also in that chorus? Has alleged honest frustration morphed into a spirit of complaint and disdain and taken up residence in our heart?

I'm sick of all these tests with a clear diagnosis. I'm sick of being asked, so what kind of work do you do. I'm sick of waiting for this house to sell... I'm sick of living in my in-law's basement... I'm sick of every time my mother visits she asks me, so just who are you, what are you doing with your life? I'm sick of being single... I'm sick of being divorced... I'm sick of this manna.

The heart is just drifting toward one complaint after another like a gravitational pull. After all it seems so reasonable; I mean look at all the disappointing events that have happened in my life... Generally, you don't have to extend an invitation for grumbling to show up-it just comes as an unwelcome guest.

You come home from yet another frustrating day only to discover that disgruntlement has moved in, unpacked its luggage, started a load of laundry, and is rifling through your refrigerator talking about making a sandwich. Try as you will to move its bags to the curb and changing the locks, its crawls back in through the windows. Complaint is a master at resisting eviction (like sin). You tell it, you don't live here, you're not welcome, you're a trespasser, go away, but it keeps coming back.

Now everyone else (in the house, on the job, in the body) is getting affected by this negative attitude. Did you know a negative attitude can expel anything positive? But here is something positive, the opposite is also true. To discourage a bad attitude and grievance from taking root in our hearts, we can invite another guest to move in—trust.

We make the conscious decision to place our confidence in God despite life's disappointments. Suddenly complaints are feeling uncomfortable.

Complaints has no one to talk to. Complaint goes to check its bags and finish unpacking for an extended stay and discovers that faith has taken all the drawers in the guest room and faith and trust have the last two seats at the table.

You see trust/faith are incompatible roommates with complaints. One pushes the other out depending on who is made to feel more at home or more comfortable. The tragedy of complaining, like with the Israelites reaction is that it undermined God's initial purpose for the whole wilderness experience. God was trying to forge or establish a relationship of trust and growth with them.

Instead, when God pulled them out of Egypt unfortunately they were more acclimated to the world of their captors than they were influenced by the character and presence of the Lord. They had not matured; they had not grown. They were an unruly group of folks who had gotten used to slavery and complaining; it was a way of life.

At least the Egyptian taskmasters were predictable. Moses, you want us to trust a God we've never even seen. We knew what to expect in Egypt and we would rather return there than follow your God. We don't even know where you're leading us. They might have been the children of Israel and the chosen ones, but they had not quite yet become the people of God. You see for that to happen there needed to be a spiritual transformation. It's rather obvious that hasn't happened yet.

This wilderness experience though well intentioned had not shaped and refined them yet into a community of trusting followers who would be prepared to enter the Promised Land. This wandering in the wilderness or "land between" was prime real estate for trust to take root and grow but you can't uproot it before it can sprout. If we're not careful some of us can become resentful and cynical and start complaining, uprooting any would-be growth.

You know the funny thing about the wilderness is, it's a great place for faith to thrive, but It is also the same desert where faith can dry up and whither in the heat.

It's ironic to hear some cliches and slogans like in painful times you hear people say, "Time heals all wounds." This isn't always true. Some people heal over time, while others allow their wounds to fester and then poison their hearts. Then they bleed off on someone else and infect them.

Choose you this day whom you will serve. Either this wilderness experience will make us bitter or make us better. Either this environment is going to make us spiritually stronger and more authentic and reliant on the Lord so we can go forth with full expectation or cause us to resent because we miss our old habits.

So what shall it be, a desert of endless wandering where we let our faith dry up or a wilderness experience where we look for and find an oasis of growth and revitalization? What shall it be, what habit shall we foster, the choice is ours. Remember Paul in the Arabia desert; he made a good choice. What shall we do? It's a new year.

God bless you,
Fwfm; nlw

Stabilizing Faith

The Lord is faithful and he will see us through every situation we can possibly imagine. The problem is when we are going via our anguish; we forget this or choose to dwell on the negative instead. We know and are familiar with Phil. 4:8, but somehow we keep vacillating to doubt. This is because we are not controlling our feelings; we're letting them control us.

Have you ever felt as if your Christian life was swinging back and forth like a pendulum? Of course you have. This is a very common problem, especially when trials come. Instead of relying on Phil. 4:8 we allow our feelings to assume control.

How long will we continue to send ourselves through these needless exercises; it's not making us stronger, it's actually zapping our strength.

Let me give you three things to consider that can determine which way our pendulum is going to swing, toward faith or toward doubt.

1. The strength of our faith or doubt at the time of trial
2. Our knowledge and understanding of the Word of God
3. Our experience with failure or success in past trials

In order to stabilize your faith it's imperative that you alter not only your focus but also your thoughts and whom you're listening to. Here are some bullet points for you. Set your mind on what God promised in His Word. It doesn't matter how impossible your situation may seem. God specializes in things thought impossible.

. Trust in the record of God; he has never failed. Remember, He has a divine nature that supersedes your feelings.
. Please remember God's ways are above our ways. View your difficulty from His perspective.
. If you're going to listen to someone let it be the Holy Spirit not Satan's murmuring lies to rile up doubt within you.
. Play back in your mind and heart over and over again how God has brought you through past trials.

By doing all of this, you chase doubt away before it can settle in you. Don't forget if you let doubt stay and get comfortable it invites friends like anxiety, fear, confusion, discouragement, and etc. Stabilize your faith by practicing these principles confirming in your life that God is faithful.

God bless you,
Fwfm.nlw

No Accident, No Luck

Do you think for a second some people just have good luck? By pure accident they just walk into good stuff. Let's look at this from a spiritual viewpoint. You see some man or woman full of grace and truth. You know they have been through sick and sin, thick and thin, but they just keep thriving right along.

Do you think this happened by accident? You already know it wasn't luck because you know they have been through hell and are still going like an Eveready battery. So what is it then?

I'll tell you what it is; they have an intimate relationship with Christ. This didn't happen accidently; it requires continual care. Decisions were made that bolstered their relationship with God so no matter what circumstances came this person kept going.

I am asking you now to reset your priorities so you can do and be better for the New Year. 2019 is saying to you; one cannot keep doing the same things and expect different results.

A great relationship doesn't just happen accidently; it takes a lot of work and dedication. Set your priorities and deliberately choose God. Stop believing you can read a book, go to a two-day conference, or have a talk with your pastor, and wham—a different life.

Knowing and seeking God is a lifetime event and it has constant competition. Day by day, week by week, month by month, and year by year. Everything and seemingly everybody attempts to keep you from becoming closer to God.

It is no "accident" and no "luck" when one can keep going after being knocked down so many times. There are those who have gone through lost jobs, lost loved ones, lost marriages, and relationships, and even lost health. Many of these folks are stronger than those who have lost nothing.

I'm asking you not to forget such a wonderful relationship with God over trivial matters or things of this world. Build an intimate relationship with God and keep it going; don't let it fizzle out like a fireplace.

God wants the best for us but we have to want the same. It takes hard work, sacrifice, and devotion. The cost of seeking the Lord is very high. Most people don't want to pay the price. You have to earnestly seek Him, making deliberate decisions, reset priorities, and refuse to do some things. You have to constantly build and build until your relationship with God is not dependent on anyone or anything like a church or group.

It is no accident and no luck; it's hard work but it's worth it. Make this a year to remember spiritually; you will not regret it.

God bless you,
Fwfm; nlw

From Whence Comes My Help…

It's a beautiful thing to have a song in your heart. My question is where did the song come from; what inspired it? Since it is a brand new year let's just think about any song that might be in our hearts. Do we hear a song because we know where God has brought us from? Do we know from whence comes our help? Are we even sober this morning? Or are we too caught up in festivities so there really is no time to praise God; we can praise Him later?

I don't know about you but I can't stop hearing the beautiful music of God's love in my heart, my mind, and my soul. It is ringing louder and louder every moment. I'm thankful that in all the shootings in random places in 2017 I was not there. There were over three thousand shootings. I was in Las Vegas at the Mandalay Bay just months before that major shooing where fifty-eight people were killed and five hundred shot.

I'm thankful for a reasonable portion of health, life and strength. I'm thankful to provide for my family. You see what I'm doing here; I'm acknowledging where my help comes from. If you are going to start your year off right, you probably should acknowledge who brought you safe thus far.

We can take a cue from the Word of Psalm 121 to help us should we not know how to praise Him.

> [1] will lift up mine eyes unto the hills from whence cometh my help.
> [2] My help cometh from the Lord, which made heaven and earth.
> [3] He will not suffer thy foot to be moved: he that keepeth thee will not slumber.

[4] Behold, he that keepeth Israel shall neither slumber nor sleep.
[5] The Lord is thy keeper: the Lord is thy shade upon thy right hand.
[6] The sun shall not smite thee by day, nor the moon by night.
[7] The Lord shall preserve thee from all evil: he shall preserve thy soul.
[8] The Lord shall preserve thy going out and thy coming in from this time forth, and even forevermore.

1. Did you know the Psalms were actually songs sang to praise God for his kindness, mercy and goodness? The Psalmist here is praising God saying he knows He is responsible for everything he has and He knows He sits high but looks low. The Psalmist is saying, Oh bless your name God for helping me even when I could not help myself; bless your name Lord, I magnify you.
2. Lord I know you made heaven and earth and look how beautiful they are. Look how you have the sun to rule the day and the moon to rule the night. Look how you separated the waters to rain and ocean; you are a magnificent God. I can look high and I can look low but I will never find another God as strong, wonderful, and mighty as you O Lord.
3. You're so good you don't allow anything in our lives that will ruin us; you're constantly warning us. You never sleep; you are always watching over us; Oh what a mighty God we serve.
4. You kept Israel and you're keeping us; thank you Lord.
5. When life becomes too sunny and hot you are our shade. I feel a song coming on here, Lord; can I just sing this Charles Wesley song.

Father, I stretch my hands to Thee, No other
help I know;
If Thou withdraw Thyself from me, Ah! Whither
shall I go?

How would my fainting soul rejoice Could I but
see Thy face
Now let me hear Thy quickening voice And taste
Thy pardoning grace

6. You see the kind of God we serve, He won't let the sun or
    moon hurt us
7. Not only so but he keeps us from evil. We don't even have
    to feel alone, forsaken, abandoned or confused; God is
    right there for us and by us and our very souls at all times.
8. Talking about going out and coming in, look at the exam-
    ple of what He did with His own Son. The life of Jesus
    coming all the way from heaven down to save a wretch
    like me. A king born in a manger; He took on the life of a
    servant to help someone He created. He lived being perse-
    cuted, beaten and ultimately put on a Roman cross. Before
    he died he said Father, forgive them for they know not
    what they do; wow!

Right in the plans, he now says, "It is finished"…He did just
what he came to do, help us. But that was not the end. For two days
he lay in that borrowed tomb that was sealed and guarded. Early on
the third day morning, our Lord got up as he said he would. He was
resurrected, but He wasn't leaving earth yet.

He walked out that tomb after folding his burial cloth and leaving it in the tomb. He was serving notice so we might understand
this folded cloth to indicate that the scene in the empty tomb was
evidence of a very calm and orderly process, rather than that of a
burglarized tomb, from which the body of Jesus was hastily stolen—
from a sealed tomb, guarded by soldiers.

Not only so Jesus didn't leave the scene, when Mary Magdalene came to the tomb and the other Mary, they did not find his body. Mary Magdalene was crying and upset and Jesus walked up to her asking her why she was crying.

You just have to read it for yourself, this is our God. (John 20:11–18)

[11] But Mary stood without at the sepulchre weeping: and as she wept, she stooped down, and looked into the sepulchre,

[12] And seeth two angels in white sitting, the one at the head, and the other at the feet, where the body of Jesus had lain.

[13] And they say unto her, Woman, why weepest thou? She saith unto them, Because they have taken away my Lord, and I know not where they have laid him.

[14] And when she had thus said, she turned herself back, and saw Jesus standing, and knew not that it was Jesus.

[15] Jesus saith unto her, Woman, why weepest thou? whom seekest thou? She, supposing him to be the gardener, saith unto him, Sir, if thou have borne him hence, tell me where thou hast laid him, and I will take him away.

[16] Jesus saith unto her, Mary. She turned herself, and saith unto him, Rabboni; which is to say, Master.

[17] Jesus saith unto her, Touch me not; for I am not yet ascended to my Father: but go to my brethren, and say unto them, I ascend unto my Father, and your Father; and to my God, and your God.

[18] Mary Magdalene came and told the disciples that she had seen the Lord, and that he had spoken these things unto her.

But wait, there's more, Jesus wasn't done yet, don't forget he still has to be ascended. He showed himself to the disciples again telling them not to go to Jerusalem until the Holy Spirit arrives. Jesus stayed around forty days before he was ascended. Everything was working according to purpose and plan.

This is where our help comes from. What a mighty God we serve. There is nothing 2018 is going to do to you that God has not ordained and will work to His purpose and your good; just look to the hills from whence comes your help.

Don't you dare look back to 2017 or beyond, but look forward and press toward the mark for the prize of the high calling of God in Christ Jesus.

God bless you,
Fwfm; nlw

Success for a New Year

> [1] Blessed is the man that walketh not in the counsel of the ungodly, nor standeth in the way of sinners, nor sitteth in the seat of the scornful. [2] But his delight is in the law of the Lord; and in his law doth he meditate day and night. (Ps. 1:1, 2)

The condition of an enlightened mind is a surrendered heart. Success is achieved by obeying God's Word. This is God's pathway, the world has its own. Which one will you follow?

What do you need to accomplish in life in order to feel successful? The truth is that our view of success is often quite different from that of God's. We think a person is successful if he or she has achieved some degree of financial security.

We look at another's material possessions and say, "He has this kind of car or she owns this type of house, therefore she he/she must be successful." Nothing is further from the truth. God defines success not by what we own or what we have materially but by whom we serve and what we do with our service.

If you are living for yourself, striving to gain a greater level of worldly recognition, or looking to add to your financial assets, the chances are you are not on the road to true success.

In our text we are given a prescription for success.... (read it in The Voice and The Message).

Stop hanging out with losers. In order to have and enjoy success, the focus of our hearts needs to be fixed on Christ. However, if the world's wants and desires drive us, we always will be left unsatisfied and longing for more.

Success is a matter of godly attitude and perspective. If yours is set on Christ, then you will experience a lifetime of true prosperity and success. Look to the right model and I can tell you now it ain't movie stars, NBA, NFL, or singers; have you looked at their lives with all their fame and money? Follow God's Word and success is yours with or without the "stuff."

God bless you,
Fwfm; nlw

Confidence in the Right Thing

1 Peter 3:10–13

You and I both know the world isn't getting any better. Aside from waxing worse as the Bible says, it is becoming extremely unstable. All of the earthquakes, pestilence, strife, natural disasters and manmade disasters are all coming to fruition just like the Bible said. There is one catastrophe after another claiming countless lives, so it would behoove us to have our confidence in the right thing.

Can you imagine putting your confidence in something you thought was solid then it crumbles; hope all your eggs were not in that basket. Too many of us are trusting people, material things and even stocks (now, why?). According to the Word, it all will be destroyed; it's just a matter of time.

There will even be a new heaven and a new earth in verse 10. So if we are wise we will put our confidence in the right thing. What is the right thing? The songwriter said, "On Christ the solid rock I stand…"

The earth is going to undergo great turmoil, more than it has already. Man is going to become even more evil, yes, more than he is now. Wouldn't it be smart to hitch your wagon to the one who is going somewhere safe? (John 14:1).

You don't have to have feelings of insecurity or fear because when you focus on the truth you can stand on that. In case you had not read this yet, Jesus is the rock of our salvation, He is a firm foundation (1 Cor. 3:10, 11; Eph. 2:20).

We service a God who is unchangeable (immutable) and sovereign; nothing can undermine or move him. He is the truth, His Word is truth, and He will last forever.

Where do you want to place your confidence; in the things of the world made by God, or in God himself?

Of course we are "in the world but we are not of the world." There will be times when we feel unsettled by our circumstances. Nevertheless we can rejoice that we know the true King of Glory and we have confidence in Him.

We should let our trials bring us even closer to his cross because it is there where we will find true peace and safety. We must be like King David who said in Psalm 16:8... My hope is built on nothing less...

The Pain of Divorce

When it comes to a permanent separation of a couple who have been married no one gets out unscathed. There will be some scars. It is never just some simple walking away and goodbye. When someone tells you it was a clean disconnection like unplugging a computer or TV, think about that; now what happens after you unplug it, right, you have no power source.

Not that your power in particular was coming from your spouse, but if you were married for any length of time and especially if you have kids, it's a hurtful operation. Someone described it as a violent act like pulling a tree out of the ground by a storm or hurricane. You can't get a divorce in the majority of cases without some damage to several people.

Now don't get me wrong, divorce may be a solution for some married issues, but in many cases it is an extreme answer to a short term problem. So many times it creates more complexities than it solves. If you ever talk to a divorcee, many of them say it was one of the most desperate and desolate periods of their life.

Not only does it cause emotional pain and turmoil but spiritually, financially, and mentally you can almost go bankrupt. Without proper counseling and reading, it is not recommended except in the most extreme cases.

Okay, I'm glad you asked. Let's explore those: adultery, physical/emotional abuse, drugs, alcohol, these are all in the extreme family. All of these issues not only ruin their own life, but if you allow them to they will also ruin yours. If you have children, you are just perpetuating the problem. Now not only are you being abused, but so are they.

Now that we have looked at the extreme cases, let's discuss the not so extreme. Irreconcilable differences, lack of motivation, lazy, finances, spiritual differences, and etc. If you get divorced for any of these reasons, you can cause more problems than you solve.

Too much attention is paid to allegedly achieving happiness, forgetting or not giving enough attention to the far reaching consequences that add up. As a result of our decision the saddest part of this is you can only get to see the awful results shattering your life and your family's life like broken glass after you have made that final break or escape as you called it.

Just like an alleged medical cure or medicine, there are unexpected side effects. Unfortunately most couples fail to see this until it is too late. It is so bad in some families until even after divorce, they get counseling and by the grace of God knit the family back together.

Divorce is so bad, so awful until God Himself said, "I hate divorce." It is a real people killer, family killer, society evil, and etc. No one sees these implications until after they have inflicted themselves with this poison of divorce.

Men become skirt chasers. Women become vulnerable and open to invitations they very well should have turned down. Many women never recover emotionally and it affects their parenting. Teens become promiscuous, hostile, and some become vandals. Many become introverted and reclusive; it just goes on and on and on. This happens all over the world no matter where you are from or what color you are. It doesn't even matter how much money you have. You cannot just undo something (for frivolous reasons) that is real and binding; it has repercussions and consequences.

The divorce percentage around the world is astonishing and very damaging. It leaves a community of very lonely, very broken people, which creates a multitude of problems. These problems consist of rebound relationships, kids being exposed to multiple strange adults coming into their alleged safe haven or home. That right there is a book in and of itself.

Where our marriage goes, in most cases so goes our morals and we justify, rationalize or excuse it by saying; I was hurting. Did you know that only one-third of homes worldwide are now functioning two parents homes? That's right, one-fourth to two-thirds homes are single parents or broken homes. Did you think you could have a broken home without broken people?

Did you think you could have dysfunctional homes without dysfunctional people; come on? The emotional distress put on adults in divorce is astronomical. Now think about the children. Think about them according to their age and sex. It ain't pretty is it? When kids are thirteen to seventeen during divorce it is the worst because they are usually close to one of their biological parents and now being ripped away from them.

Now you want them to like someone else whom they don't even know and who is no kin to them. Then there are the little children; they don't even know what hit them. They don't understand what is taking place, where they are going to live, where they are going to go to school, and etc. It is easier for them than teenagers because of their innocence but they are none the less fractured, and they too are victims. it can get so confusing for kids until they don't know who to turn to for emotional support and help. Too many of them turn to each other and that is must disastrous.

Of course while all of this is taking place everyone is getting older. These issues and their related counterparts like drinking, drugs, promiscuity, confusion, and so on, is taken right into adulthood. Now you have these kids who become adults and have new marriage relationships pending that have little chance of being successful because they themselves are not even healed from their wounds.

God bless you,
Fwfm: nlw

I Still Believe

No matter who we are or where we are from we are going to have our issues. Of course some people's troubles will be greater than those of others. May I remind you that no matter what the difficulty, we must all continue to trust God. Some of us have lost loved ones, some have lost spouses; some have lost jobs, and some of us have lost our mind. Let me tell you, whatever the difficulty we must continue to trust God.

The other day in Santa Monica a man for whatever reason killed his family then randomly started shooting people in cars and at the Santa Monica College nearby. Innocent people were gunned down just for being on the road and at school. It could have been you or I.

I'm reminded of a man who lost his teenage daughter in an auto accident. She was leaving summer camp one day and had an accident on the way home. Can you even imagine this happening to you? At the camp, one of the songs she used to sing was "I Still Believe." I wonder if you can just let this story bless you right now.

Though the questions still fog up my mind with promises I still seem to bear; even when answers slowly unwind. It's my heart I see you prepare. But it's now that I feel your grace fall like the rain; from every anger tip washing away my pain.

> Cause I still believe in Your faithfulness
> Cause I still believe in Your faithfulness
> Cause I still believe in Your Holy Word
> Even when I don't see, I still believe.

This, my friend, is the measure of it all. When it comes to our troubles; you must say, "I still believe." You must claim the very remarkable and hopeful words of (2 Cor 6:4–10, NIV). [4] Rather, as servants of God we commend ourselves in every way: in great endurance; in troubles, hardships and distresses;5 in beatings, imprisonments and riots; in hard work, sleepless nights and hunger;

> [6] in purity, understanding, patience and kindness; in the Holy Spirit and in sincere love;
> [7] in truthful speech and in the power of God; with weapons of righteousness in the right hand and in the left;
> [8] through glory and dishonor, bad report and good report; genuine, yet regarded as impostors;
> [9] known, yet regarded as unknown; dying, and yet we live on; beaten, and yet not killed;
> [10] sorrowful, yet always rejoicing; poor, yet making many rich; having nothing, and yet possessing everything.

Yes, you will go through some stuff, plenty of stuff. "In this world you will have tribulations…" (John 16:33). Google it.

You have God's Word on it, you must still believe.

God bless you,
Fwfm: nlw

Seasoning Salt

The fact that a location or place is rich in beauty such as landscaping, trees, and fruits are a good thing. A church, a home, a marriage, should all have some rich soil and good fruit. Here in Jericho, it was an oasis of rich soil, palms, pomegranates, and fig trees even though it was in the desert.

So just because your region is hot and dry it doesn't mean you still can't produce good things. Just because you work around heathens or live around questionable folk doesn't mean you still can't be good and have good things come from your marriage or from your house, your family.

There was a problem in Jericho that was so bad it was believed to be able to ruin everything that was good. The spring had become toxic and now the crops were sterile/barren. Baal worship had taken over Israel. It was now the state religion. How did this occur; the former Queen Jezebel was an ardent student of the craft, so she established Baal sites all over Jezreel, Israel's summer capitol. She supported over 450 Baal priests and induced her husband King Ahab to build large shrines in Samaria to house great crowds of Baal worshippers.

We're talking groves, shrines, temples, and Baal consorts, dotted the landscape while Jezebels priest poisoned the minds of her people with lies and false teaching. Baal was considered the god who governed the water and soil, the fertility god. He was the god of the crops and rain. Of course he was only a piece of manmade rock...

Isn't it ironic that today we have gotten away from all things family? No more board games (Monopoly, Scattergory, Bingo, and etc.). No these are boring; yes it kept the family together but we have moved on. Even when TV came along, at first it was all family shows like *I Love Lucy*, they didn't even sleep in the same bed, *Remember*

Andy Griffin, Father Knows Best, That Girl, Flying Nun, all family shows? Divorce rate was at about 8 percent. Suddenly TV got aggressive, we needed to see some flesh, and talk dirty. We even needed to have unnatural affection plastered all over the screen. (*Baywatch, Two Men and a Baby, Glee*). Every picture now was mandated by gay ALCU to have a gay in it or be protested. Everyone complied, even the churches…

Well, the water, the spring, became bad. Divorce went to 50 percent even in the church. Prayer was taken out of schools; mass shootings occurred. The family disintegrated. It was now called broken homes or dysfunctional families. It became the norm that as soon as there was anything you didn't like, flee, run. Never mind the investment in the corporation to the CEO, COO, or Board. The board is expendable; oh, the water was bad. It sterilized the family; it made the family barren.

Now the family is two men and a baby, two women and a baby. Now we're producing boys who like boys, girls who like girls, oh this is some bad water. We need a prophet; we need to have this water cleansed. Even the so-called church was drinking the water. In the Catholic Church Priests molesting little boys, preachers sleeping with their pew or laity, and nobody stopped it. Oh there was some murmuring (isn't that a shame) but they still went right down to the temple, to the mass, to Double Rock COGIC and put in their offering.

One woman who knew the married pastor had a girlfriend in the church that was on paid staff said, "I know, but no church is perfect." I just need a traditional Black Community Church." Her family since was contaminated/ruined from drinking the bad water.

Oh, God, we need a prophet! Second Kings 2:19: Elisha, our water is pretty bad, can you help us? Verse 20: All right, bring me a new bowl and fill it with salt. A new (new wine, new wineskins), bowl represented a new thing, a new way. Never mind your tradition, you see where it has landed us. There's a new prophet in town, this Baal worship has got to go.

Then salt, why salt, salt was a purifying agent, a cleansing agent, it was used to disinfect. Remember Jesus said we're the salt of the earth…? Remember Paul said in Col. 4:6…seasoned with salt. 6 Let your conversation be always full of grace, seasoned with salt, so that you may know how to answer everyone.

Elisha took the new bowl filled with salt and went right to the source of water, the spring, the city well, and threw the salt in the well. (You want to clean something up; you have to start at the source of the contamination.) Then he declared, "The Lord has healed these waters, they shall no longer cause death or barren land."

In order to clean up you have to go to the source of the bad. Satan's minions had ruined the land bringing sterility to everything God created and loved. Elisha's business was to undo this malicious intent and deadly influence and teach others how to do it. Elisha wanted the young prophets to know your battle is not against flesh and blood… (Eph. 6:12). If anything was to be done it had to be done in the invisible realm of the Spirit. So Elisha preached this symbolic message: "Seasoning Salt," bring me some salt.

Don't you know the power God has given each of us 2 Cor. 4:7?

The Word exudes from us, the life we live, our family, our clarity, we are the salt of the earth. It's not about us: it's about God in us.

And I, brethren, when I came to you, did not come with excellence of speech or of wisdom declaring to you the testimony of God. 2 For I determined not to know anything among you except Jesus Christ and Him crucified. I was with you in weakness, in fear, and in much trembling. 4 And my speech and my preaching were not with persuasive words of human wisdom, but in demonstration of the Spirit and of power, When God speaks miraculous things begin to happen. Memories are cleansed, passions are purified, bitter hearts are sweetened, and souls are seasoned with beauty and grace. Marriages are saved, families are put back together, oh the Word, the seasoning salt, doesn't return void. It will accomplish what He desired and achieve the purpose for which He sends it. (1 Cor. 2:1 3, 4)

It's not about the prophet's ability to express, it rests solely on God's Word. It's God Himself speaking to us. "For this reason we also thank God without ceasing, because when you received the word of God which you heard from us, you welcomed it not as the word of men, but as it is in truth, the word of God, which also effectively works in you who believe" (1 Thes. 2:13).

> So shall My word be that goes forth from My mouth;
> It shall not return to Me void,
> But it shall accomplish what I please,
> And it shall prosper in the thing for which I sent it. (Isa. 55:11)
>
> He's sweet I know
> The waters are still sweet to this day…

God bless you,
Fwfm: nlw

Temperament, Rejection, Failure

Psalm 25:1, 2 16, 21 (look it up).

A melancholy person can be a danger to himself and those around him. Unfortunately one who is depressed spends a lot of time reflecting inward looking and self-appraising from a negative standpoint. Introspection is good, but it must be balanced. To spend an inordinate amount of time photographing one's emotional state and then developing the film is not productive.

I do realize none of us are responsible for the temperament we inherited; however we are responsible for the way we react or control our temperament. Do not believe for a second that you are caught in some grip and are a slave to your feelings. Do not fail in spiritual matters and use the excuse that, "Well, that's just how I am."

You really do need to distinguish between what is temperament and what is deliberate. I am well aware there are involuntary emotions that sometimes overtake us, but our executive deciders (our will, our mind) have to make a choice.

It cannot be always about how we feel; we must choose via our mind and will what is best for us. Remember we are what we choose.

We cannot and we must not give in to being distant, withdrawn, and temperamental lest we intentionally want to be a very lonely person. Have you noticed people who are excessively demanding, need constant affection no matter how much they get, are overly possessive or jealous? These kinds of folks want to have exclusive use of whoever they are with. I say this because there are self-confidence issues.

It's not that they are being rejected or abandoned; they just feel they are and it set's them off. These are the kind of folk who feel condemned even though no one said anything or very little. It's their temperament. Unfortunately they see the darker side of life rather than the brighter. To them the glass is half empty instead of half full.

So this fear of being rejected is real to them. It doesn't help when they hear no to a loan, or no to a relationship, or no to being accepted by a college or group or club. They take this personal. They can become cold and sensitive because they are putting up a buffer against future rejection. Many times without even thinking, they retreat into one's self to avoid being hurt again.

Many times temperamental people don't want to try anything new because they don't want to take the chance of failure. They don't want to go forward in a relationship because it's easier to give up due to feeling like a failure. This kind of thinking can handicap one for life, but this is the life of many people.

An increasing number of Christians including leaders and pastors are finding themselves in these temperamental positions. It is causing the breakdown in marriages, families, and churches. Many try to hide it but it rears its ugly head and bobs up and pokes a husband/wife or friend without cause.

It can only be concealed for so long. Of course when temperamental people do make a legitimate error or commit a sin they have difficulty accepting that. It can cause them severe depression. They withdraw and become even more melancholy.

Look at David in Psalm 32:3–5.

So what does one do when you are temperamental, feeling rejected and allergic to failure? You do what David did in Ps. 32, confess it to God.

There will be a shout of joy and release when you acknowledge where you stand. Tell God all about, it will make you easier to get along with. It will also break you out of the isolated state these negative feelings have backed you into.

God bless you,
Fwfm; nlw

About the Author

Naum L. Ware has been a Baptist minister for forty years. He started out as a policeman and nine months later was called into the ministry. Naum had a very successful police career for twenty-three years. Doing that same time he pastored as a senior pastor and youth pastor in Long Beach California and Pasadena, California. Naum has been a marriage counselor for thirty-five years and ran Marriage Class 101–401 for over thirty years with various churches in the Los Angeles area.

It was through all of these experiences from the world and from the church that Naum could put together such an array of encouragement. When you arrest people and minister to people you get to know what their needs are. This is on top of a forty-year marriage to Annette Ware with two children who are now thirty-nine and thirty-seven. Naum Jr. is a police sergeant with LAPD and Nicole is a psychologist.

Between family counseling in church and in the field, also raising a family and pastoring numerous people you can't help but garner ways to encourage, uplift, and edify others to keep them on the right path.

CPSIA information can be obtained
at www.ICGtesting.com
Printed in the USA
FSHW021552220319
56589FS